Manipulation:

The Most Powerful Techniques to Influencing People, Persuasion, Mind Control, Reading People, NLP. How to Analyze People and Mind Control.

Table of Contents

Introduction

Chapter One: Emotional Manipulation ... 25

Chapter Two: Covert Manipulation Techniques ... 41

Chapter Three: NLP Manipulation Techniques ... 59

Chapter Four: Persuading and Influencing People ... 72

Chapter Five: Tackling Manipulation in Relationships ... 102

Chapter Six: Manipulating Mass Opinion as a Public Speaker ... 113

Chapter Seven: Manipulating With Small-Talk ... 120

Conclusion ... 149

© Copyright 2019 by Tony Bennis - All rights reserved.

This Book is provided with the sole purpose of providing relevant information on a specific topic for which every reasonable effort has been made to ensure that it is both accurate and reasonable. Nevertheless, by purchasing this Book you consent to the fact that the author, as well as the publisher, are in no way experts on the topics contained herein, regardless of any claims as such that may be made within. As such, any suggestions or recommendations that are made within are done so purely for entertainment value. It is recommended that you always consult a professional prior to undertaking any of the advice or techniques discussed within.

This is a legally binding declaration that is considered both valid and fair by both the Committee of Publishers Association and the American Bar Association and should be considered as legally binding within the United States.

The reproduction, transmission, and duplication of any of the content found herein, including any specific or extended information will be done as an illegal act regardless of the end form the information ultimately takes. This includes copied versions of the work both physical, digital and audio unless express consent of the Publisher is provided beforehand. Any additional rights reserved.

Furthermore, the information that can be found within the pages described forthwith shall be considered both accurate and truthful when it comes to the recounting of facts. As such, any use, correct or incorrect, of the provided information will render the Publisher free of responsibility as to the actions taken outside of their direct purview. Regardless, there are zero scenarios where the original author or the Publisher can be deemed liable in any fashion for any damages or hardships that may result from any of the information discussed herein.

Additionally, the information in the following pages is intended only for informational purposes and should thus be thought of as universal. As befitting its nature, it is presented without assurance regarding its prolonged validity or interim quality. Trademarks that are mentioned are done without written consent and can in no way be considered an endorsement from the trademark holder.

Introduction

Ever wondered how some people can always get others to do what they want them to, irrespective of whether the other person wants to do it or not. There is an unspoken almost hypnotic quality that sways people to take the intended action. It can be their words, body language, voice, sneaky strategies or a combination of all. The bottom line- they always have people eating out of their hands and doing what they want them to. While we've all manipulated people in one way or the other in varying degrees throughout our life, some people have mastered the art of manipulating, influencing and persuading people to take the desired action.

While things look all rose-tinted and beautiful on the outside, even with an ideal upbringing, great education and a stellar career, we've all been victims of unsavory tactics used by people to have their way by preying on our feelings, self-worth, and emotions. We've all been part of manipulative relationships where the strings of our feelings and emotions were cleverly controlled by another person to fulfill their needs.

While humans at large thrive on love, kindness, and gratitude, it cannot be denied that it self-centered species. Yes, we are self-serving by nature! While you may not think being selfish or self-serving is a negative trait. Why shouldn't we think about ourselves? However, some folks that this self-centeredness too far. In their bid to serve their needs, they tread upon the feelings and emotions of others.

When people start resorting to intentional, calculated and cunning techniques for having their way is what makes it evil. The intensity of this may vary from person to person depending on their upbringing, environment, personality, experiences, education and several other factors.

We all are guilty of using manipulation at some point, often without realizing it. In the same vein, we are often manipulated by people close to us without realizing that we are being victims of manipulation. And this is precisely what makes it so sinister and insidious. We are made to think, feel and act in a specific way to fulfill another person's need without consideration for our emotions.

For instance, you may be made to feel guilty about working hard or putting in long hours of work even though you are doing it to build a future for your loved ones. Or you'll be made to feel like you are an irresponsible person for taking a break from housework and letting your hair down with friends.

The stark reality about manipulation is that it originates from people who are grappling with issues related to security, self-confidence, and comfort. They attempt to push their luck in a bid to hold other people down for fear of losing them. Manipulators operate from a deep sense of insecurity. Ironically, what they don't realize is in their bid to hold people down owing to the fear of losing them, they end doing just that. Losing people!

Other times, manipulators are simply out to take advantage of people to serve their cut throat, selfish purposes. They are cold, calculating and ruthless in their acts. There is no regard for the feelings and emotions of their victims. It is a 'dog eat dog' world according to them, and to survive they believe they have to use other people.

Manipulators operate with a point of view that they have to reach their end through whatever means it takes, and if it ends up hurting a few people along the way, so be it. These are people who should actively watch out for and avoid.

The purpose of this book is to make you aware of the sneaky tricks people use for manipulating others. It aims to uncover how people use emotional manipulation, mind control, and persuasion to fulfill their self needs.

When you are able to identify clever manipulative techniques, it becomes easier to guard against them. You'll learn to read warning signs of manipulation and use practical techniques to safeguard your emotions and self-confidence, thus accomplishing complete immunity against people's sly tactics.

Manipulation is starkly different from persuasion. While persuasion awards the other person a right to select his/her response to a particular situation, manipulation does give the victim the right to choice. Manipulation has only one way – the way your manipulator wants you to take. There is only a single 'correct choice': the manipulators choice. There is zero regards or concern for your wishes, desires, choices, and emotions. You will pay with hell if you don't pick the choice they want you to.

Typical manipulative tactics include

-Complaining

-Playing victim

-Inducing guilt

-Comparing

-Offering excuses and rationalizing

-Feigning ignorance

-Emotional blackmail

-Evasiveness

-Demonstrating fake concern

-Undermining people

-Blaming others and using "who me?" defenses

-Lying

-Denying

-False flattery

-Intimidation

-Giving the illusion of selflessness

-Shaming

- Using foot in the door techniques

and more

Ever wondered how some people can get others to do exactly what they want? Or how they garner a large following of folks who are more than eager to agree with them or follow their instructions? What are the secret life skills that these people use in the real world to influence people and get them to agree to things?

Mastering the fine art of winning and influencing people is an asset for life. It allows you to bring the best out of others, encourages them to see things from your perspective and ultimately helps them do exactly what you want them to.

It is important to understand that none of the techniques described in the book falls under the dark art strategies of persuading people. Influencing people isn't about destroying their self-esteem to feel great about self.

Au contraire, it is about building them up by encouraging and inspiring them. There are multiple psychological strategies to influence people without making them feel miserable about themselves. We take a hugely positive and constructive approach when it comes to being an amazing influencer and influencing people in the right direction.

Wonder why some influencers inspire a following that goes all out to please them while others can barely get people to acknowledge their instructions? It is about building a connection that drives people in the right direction. Much as pop psychology writers wouldn't want you to believe this, influencing people is more than a bunch of psychological tricks. It runs deeper into people's emotions, their subconscious minds, and their most compelling motivators.

According to a legend doing the rounds, Benjamin Franklin had once wanted to please a man who didn't like him much. He went ahead and asked the man to lend him (Franklin) a rare publication. When Franklin received it, he went ahead and thanked the man graciously. The result – the two become great friends.

In Franklin's own words, "He that has once done kindness will be more ready to do you another than he whom you yourself have obliged." Seemingly small acts like (saying a thank you or being gracious) these go a long way in forging bonds where people truly like you and listen to you.

Have you heard of conversation hypnosis? The term has gained much momentum recently and is nothing but a series of techniques used for subconsciously influencing an individual or group's behavior in such as way that they believe their opinion has changed with their own will.

Of course, this area of persuading/ influencing people falls in the grey zone. Influencing people with them believing that it is through their volition can be misleading. It is for every individual to determine whether they want to use these tricks ethically or no. However, there are plenty of proven white-hat techniques to get you started with talking and behaving in a way that makes people sit up and take note.

Effective communication forms the basis of both – your personal and professional encounters. The words, actions, and gestures you use to connect with people help them understand you and make it easier for you to influence their actions in your favor.

Influencing people subtly is all about being a powerful communicator, charismatic influencer and persuasive individual. There are tons of ways through which you can get people to agree with you without being argumentative or negative. This book tells you how. It helps you understand how people react to different stimuli, what drives them to do what they do and how to encourage/inspire them in positive ways. Let's get started right away.

Now that you are fairly competent in identifying emotional and covert manipulation tactics, let's understand what leads people to manipulate others. This may help you deal with them more efficiently.

We've all been victims of everything from pathological lying to being made to feel inadequate to suffering awful smear campaigns. They are beyond reasonable standards of human behavior. What makes people turn into sinister manipulators? What leads manipulators to use the tactics they do? What makes them defy norms of human behavior and turn to underhand techniques to have their way with people?

Manipulation is a double edged sword with largely negative connotations. However, in certain circumstances, it can also be used to meet a positive end purpose when no other straight tactic is effective. This handbook of manipulation will not just give you a treasure of manipulation and persuasion tips but also tips for dealing with manipulators in daily life and especially interpersonal relationships. I've taken a comprehensive view of manipulation as a hammer that can be used to destroy things or hit a nail on the wall. Think of it as a powerful tool – you can either use it to build something or destroy it. How you use manipulation is in your hands. While on one hand, you are offered a bunch of manipulation techniques to influence people, on the other, there are tips to safeguard you against sinister or negative manipulation.

Read on to get deeper insights about what makes people manipulate others in ways you'd never imagine.

Why do people manipulate?

Manipulators are constantly living under fear and insecurity. What if this doesn't happen? What if my partner leaves me for someone else? What if someone gains an upper hand over me? They want to win and control all the time to combat an inherent sense of fear.

Where does this fear steam from? It originates from a deep sense of unworthiness. This simply translates as I am certainly not worthy of the good things and people in life, hence these things and people will leave me. To prevent them from leaving me, I must resort to some underhand techniques that will give me absolute control over the people and things I believe I don't deserve. In short, the underlying message is – I am undeserving or unworthy of people and things!

Fear

Why does a person use manipulation to fulfill his/her own agenda? Simple, fear!

It is obvious that manipulators fear that will never be able to gain the desired outcome on their own abilities. That if they act ethically, people and life will not rally reward them positively. They operate from the view that people are life and people are positioned against them. Manipulators fear everyone as their enemy and believe life will not necessarily be favorable to them if they act favorably.

There is a fear that resources are limited and if they don't gain something, others will. They think it's a dog eat dog universe where people have to controlled to help them accomplish the desired result. This control can be in any form – emotional, psychological, financial or practical. They want to control people so they can achieve their desired agenda and out their fear to rest.

Low or No Conscience

Lack of consciousness is another fundamental reason for manipulation. When a person fails to realize that he/she is responsible for their own reality, there is a greater tendency to operate without a conscience. Manipulators don't believe a fair system exists. Also, they've stopped evolving. They don't learn from earlier experiences or try to accomplish a state of congruence between inner emotions and external life.

The view manipulation as a safe or secure world for getting the desired result, despite the fact that these results have not brought them satisfaction in the past. Emotionally and psychologically they keep coming back to square one from time to time, never learning their lesson. To avoid this lesson, they will create another reason to manipulate. Thus, they are caught in a vicious circle of unworthiness or dissatisfaction and then creating another manipulation need.

Manipulation doesn't pay beyond the initial brief fix since the manipulative action is not an authentic, balanced or effective. It is a defense reaction to perceived hurt, unworthiness, fear or insecurity. By being manipulative, the person is attempting to offset these emotions.

Manipulation is a deliberate act that is not aligned with a person's conscience or the greater good. The person doesn't operate with a "we are one" understanding, which means he/she seeks to gain through manipulation by authenticity rather than non-authenticity. Anything gained through non authenticity only leads to narrow victories, ongoing trouble, emptiness or fear, and unworthiness. This creates an even bigger sense of unworthiness. Again unworthiness is a fear of not being worthy of others love and acceptance.

Manipulative folks do not learn, evolve or realize the power of authenticity. Lack of realization of the real power of authenticity and worthiness comes from knowing that one is cherished and accepted for what they really are. In essence, a feeling of unworthiness is often at the core of manipulation.

They Don't Want To Pay The Price Attached to Reach Their Goals

People often manipulate to serve their needs because they do not want to pay the price attached to their goal. They often strive to accomplish the objective or serve their purpose without wanting to give back or pay the price in return.

For instance, if you don't want your partner to leave you, the relationship will take work. You'll have to give your partner love, compassion, understanding, time, loyalty, encouragement, inspiration, a secure future and much more.

A manipulator may not want his/her, partner, to leave them but they don't want to pay the price of maintaining a happy, secure and healthy relationship, where the partner will never leave them.

They may not want to be loyal or spend much time with their partner, and yet expect them to stay. When people are not ready to pay the price of accomplishing what they want, they may resort to manipulation or underhand techniques to achieve these goals without paying the price attached to them.

Similarly, if a manipulative person wants to be promoted in his/her workplace, rather than working hard, staying past work hours, upgrading their skills or getting a degree, they will simply manipulate their way into the position. The person is not prepared to pay the price or do what it takes to be promoted.

At times, it's deeply ingrained in a person's psyche that wants are bad or that he/she shouldn't have any desires since it makes them come across as selfish. Manipulation then becomes a way to get what they desire or need without even asking for it.

Manipulators realize there is a price attached to everything. A person won't do them a favor without expecting a favor in return. They won't keep getting things if they don't demonstrate kindness and gratitude. A person won't love them or have sex with them without getting commitment, loyalty, and love in return. Manipulators try to push their luck by trying to get something without paying the price attached to it. It is often an easy way out.

They Think They Won't Get Caught

Another reason people manipulate is that they think they can get away with their sneaky acts and that the victims won't realize they are being manipulated. They are also confident that the victim can't do anything even if they manipulation cover is blown.

What gives manipulators the feeling that they won't be caught? Some people come across as inherently clueless, vulnerable, insecure and naïve. These are the type of people manipulators prey on. They believe a person who has low confidence, a low sense of self-worth or is clueless about the ways of the world is less likely to figure out that he/she is being manipulated.

Also, manipulators know that in the event that their manipulation cover is blown, the victim will not be able to do much. They cleverly pick targets who are low on confidence, self-acceptance, body image or sense of self worth. It is easier to play on the vulnerabilities of these people than assertive and self-assure people who won't allow people to take advantage of them.

For example, say a person has low awareness of social dynamics, doesn't understand jokes easily, doesn't identify a prank early, is unable to differentiate between genuine courtesy and sexual advances, can't tell when someone is genuinely attracted to them or simply wants to go to bed with them and other similar social and interpersonal dynamics are likelier to be manipulated.

Manipulators are well aware that their victims can't do anything if they don't even realize that their weaknesses are being misused. They often cash in on the cluelessness of their victims by saying they are imaging things or making something up. An already clueless and unsure person is less likely to question this idea. When you are already reeling under feelings of insecurity, cluelessness, and vulnerability, how difficult is it for the manipulator to take advantage of these feelings by reinforcing them further? Manipulators

Manipulators manipulate because they think they can hurt or upset their victims more than the victims can hurt or upset them. They will almost always target people who come across as nice and vulnerable. When people are oblivious to the dishonesty existing within social relationships, they aren't really accustomed to dishonest allegiances. This doesn't equip them with the means to confront or counter dishonesty, which makes them less aware of being manipulated.

They Aren't Able to Accept Their Shortcomings

When people are unable to come to terms with their shortcomings or do not accept the responsibility or accountability for the faults, there is an inherent need to make others feel lesser than them.

If manipulators aren't good enough or feel miserable about themselves, there is a desire to make others feel equally worthless or miserable about themselves. When a person believes he/she is unworthy of someone, they will manipulate the person to feel unworthy too so that they can then gain control over his/her perception that they need the manipulator in their life to feel worthy. By putting others down or gaining control over others, they experience a form of pseudo superiority. If they can't be good enough for others, let's make others feel like they aren't good enough too to retain control over them.

In effect, manipulators don't want their victims to realize that they (the manipulators) aren't good enough or unworthy of them (the victims). The manipulator will therefore carefully cultivate a feeling of helplessness and unworthiness within the victim to keep them hooked to him/her. If a person realizes that he/she is more attractive, intelligent, richer, capable, efficient, self-sufficient, etc., the higher will be their chances of leaving the manipulator. On the other hand, if the manipulator injects a feeling of them not being 'complete', they'll need someone to 'complete' them.

Manipulators are not able to accept their shortcomings or deal with criticism. They are often grappling with deep psychological issues or insecurities. By manipulating others, they do not have to confront their own insecurities to feel higher than others. For someone operating with such a narrow perspective, even a little correction, feedback or criticism can seem like a huge defeat.

People who manipulate don't know how to deal with defeat. When you hesitate to give feedback because the person will get defensive or blow things out of proportion or won't take things in the right spirit, it may be a sign you are dealing with someone who can't come to terms with criticism.

Notice how manipulators will seldom express feelings of gratitude of thankfulness. They find it challenging to be grateful to others because in their view by doing so they are increasing their sense of being obligated to another person, which doesn't give them an upper hand in any relationship.

For example, if you do someone a huge favor, they feel obliged to return that favor which puts you above them in the relationship dynamics until they return the favor. Manipulators don't want to give you the upper hand by feeling obliged to you. Therefore, they will demonstrate minimal gratefulness so you don't believe you've done something huge for them or that they are obliged to you. The idea is to always be one-up on you and this feel of being indebted to you doesn't make them feel one-up.

Avoiding accepting your shortcomings

When people are unable to come to terms with their shortcomings or do not accept the responsibility or accountability for the faults, there is an inherent need to make others feel lesser than them.

If manipulators aren't good enough or feel miserable about themselves, there is a desire to make others feel equally worthless or miserable about themselves. When a person believes he/she is unworthy of someone, they will manipulate the person to feel unworthy too so that they can then gain control over his/her perception that they need the manipulator in their life to feel worthy. By putting others down or gaining control over others, they experience a form of pseudo superiority. If they can't be good enough for others, let's make others feel like they aren't good enough too to retain control over them.
In effect, manipulators don't want their victims to realize that they (the manipulators) aren't good enough or unworthy of them (the victims). The manipulator will therefore carefully cultivate a feeling of helplessness and unworthiness within the victim to keep them hooked to him/her. If a person realizes that he/she is more attractive, intelligent, richer, capable, efficient, self-sufficient, etc., the higher will be their chances of leaving the manipulator. On the other hand, if the manipulator

injects a feeling of them not being 'complete', they'll need someone to 'complete' them.

Manipulators are not able to accept their shortcomings or deal with criticism. They are often grappling with deep psychological issues or insecurities. By manipulating others, they do not have to confront their own insecurities to feel higher than others. For someone operating with such a narrow perspective, even a little correction, feedback or criticism can seem like a huge defeat.

People who manipulate don't know how to deal with defeat. When you hesitate to give feedback because the person will get defensive or blow things out of proportion or won't take things in the right spirit, it may be a sign you are dealing with someone who can't come to terms with criticism.

Notice how manipulators will seldom express feelings of gratitude of thankfulness. They find it challenging to be grateful to others because in their view by doing so they are increasing their sense of being obligated to another person, which doesn't give them an upper hand in any relationship.

For example, if you do someone a huge favor, they feel obliged to return that favor which puts you above them in the relationship dynamics until they return the favor. Manipulators don't want to give you the upper hand by feeling obliged to you. Therefore, they will demonstrate minimal gratefulness so you don't believe you've done something huge for them or that they are obliged to you. The idea is to always be one-up on you and this feel of being indebted to you doesn't make them feel one-up.

Chapter One: Emotional Manipulation

While everyone is guilty of using manipulation (knowingly or unknowingly) at some point, what makes emotional manipulators different is they habitually trample upon people's emotions and feelings to serve their own selfish needs. It is a way of life for some people to use other people's feelings in a bid to increase their psychological hold or superiority over the person.

1. Play on people's fears. Emotional manipulators tend to blow facts out of proportion and highlight only specific points in a bid to instill fear in you. For example, a man who doesn't want his wife to pursue a full-time career outside the house may tell her something like "research reveals 60 percent of all divorces happen when both partners are engaged in full-time careers", sneakily hiding the fact that there can be reasons other than the woman's career or job. This is cleverly constructed to prey on the woman's fear of losing the relationship is she gives in to her ambitions.

2. The actions and words shouldn't match. Emotional manipulators tell you exactly what they think you want to hear but will rarely follow it up with action. They will pledge commitment and support. However, when it comes to act upon their commitment they will make you feel guilty for coming up with unreasonable demands.

At one point they'll tell you how fortunate they are to know a person like you, and the next they'll be slamming you for being a burden. This is a clever tactic for undermining a person's belief about their sanity. Emotional manipulators will keep saying things that suit their purpose and suddenly mold a perception to the contrary by doing the opposite of what they said to misbalance sanity.

This also comes at a price, which they'll sneakily claim in future. As an emotional manipulator, you are constantly reminding people about how you helped them and use that as leverage to make them feel obliged to you. If you perpetually remind them of a favor you willingly did for them, which makes the other person feel they owe you something, there are high chances you are being emotionally manipulated.

3. Become masters at distributing guilt. Few people leverage the power of guilt like practiced manipulators. Emotional manipulators induce guilt in other people to serve their needs. If someone brings up an issue that's been bothering them for discussion, manipulators make them feel guilty about feeling the way they do, however, justified these feelings may seem. Emotional manipulators make people feel guilty for mentioning the issue. When someone doesn't mention the issue, make you feel miserable for not being open and talking about it.

Keep stewing guilt in you, irrespective of the direction of the other person's thoughts and actions. One way or another, find reasons to make you feel guilty. Anything they choose to do is wrong. Irrespective of the problems the other person may be having collectively, an emotional manipulator will always make them feel it is only your fault. Manipulators blame people for everything unfortunate happening in their life and build a strong sense of guilt within them. If you want to get people to do what you want them to, induce a sense of guilt and regret. Guilt is one of the strongest manipulation forces that drive people to delve deep and give in to what you want them to.

Emotional manipulators prey on their victims by posing themselves to be the victims. They lead their victims into believing that it is always their fault irrespective of whether they are truly responsible or not. The blame is always assigned to the victim with the manipulator playing the victim. This is done in effect to move responsibility from the manipulator's shortcomings to blaming the victim, which is done with the intention of inducing guilt in them. When a victim feels a sense of guilt of self-blame for the unpleasant situation, it becomes simpler for the manipulator to get them to take the desired action.

Manipulators concentrate on how the other person got them to do something or how it is the other person's fault for which they (the manipulators) are suffering. It is always the other person who is making the manipulator angry, hurt and upset. As a manipulator, you seldom accept accountability or responsibility for your own actions.

Let us consider an example here to illustrate this emotional manipulation strategy even more effectively. Your partner is upset with you for forgetting your anniversary. The reasonable thing to do in such a scenario would be to apologize for the goof up and make it up to them later by giving them a surprise or a nice gift. However, manipulators resort to playing blame games. The blame is turned on its head in the direction of the other person. You make the other person feel guilty about making you feel so terrible about forgetting an anniversary. There is a tendency to introduce a sense of guilt so the other person can do what you want them to.

So to justify forgetting your anniversary to your partner and inducing a sense of guilt, you may speak about how stressed, tired, busy and exhausted you have been, and how inconsiderate it is on their part to blame you for forgetting an anniversary when you've been working really hard on a project lately. We have in effect made the other person feel guilty for a reasonable expectation. The tables are being turned on them to avoid taking on the blame of forgetting the anniversary.

Hardcore manipulators will not stop there, however, and instead they will go one step further, and go over all the instances when the other person has forgotten important occasions in a bid to justify their own forgetfulness. You make the other person feel like it is indeed their fault for expecting you to remember all dates when you are stressed with work. It acts as a sort of justification for your forgetfulness. Master manipulators know how to weave a sense of guilt within the other person's consciousness to lead them into taking the intended action. They use blame and guilt generously to fulfill their needs.

For instance, let us assume an individual brings up something that is working on their mind for a long time now. Manipulators will most probably make them feel like they are making a mountain out of a molehill, and that it isn't a big deal. You make the other person feel guilty about making an issue out of a seemingly non-issue. Rather than accepting their troubles and committing to work on them, the tables are turned on the other person to make them feel guilty for mentioning the issue or their true feelings. This manipulation technique is primarily used in personal relationships when one person opens up to the other partner, and the latter turns back and blames him/her for bringing up something so trivial.

You make the other person feel guilty about everything they do. If they remain silent, you may accuse them of not sharing their feelings or not trusting you with a resolution for their problems. If they happen to share their feelings, you blame them for making issues where there are none. There is constant guilt stirring to make the other person feel that they are always at fault to meet your own agenda.

All the other person's actions are attributed to him/her or presented/positioned as their fault until they meet your agenda. At the same time, you don the role of the unfortunate victim. Inducing a sense of guilt is, in fact, one of the most powerful manipulation strategies for getting someone to obey you. This becomes even more effective on folks who suffer from low self-esteem or reduced self-confidence levels.

For example, if you want to get someone to take the desired action, confidently rattle off a list of favors you've done for them or all the instances when you have gone out of the way to help them. Later, follow this by how you've felt let down every time you've expected something from them. You turn into a projected victim who did all the wonderful things to help them out in their time of need, and they turn into the ungrateful beings that do not stand up to your needs when required. This is subtly playing on the victims' minds to make them think like they are not returning the favor or being thankless.

Manipulators often get the other person to do what they want by saying something like, "It is fine Roger, I cannot expect anything more from you. It is really my fault that I keep expecting a lot from you and our relationship. This induces a sense of guilt in the other person as if he/she is letting the manipulator down, which may or may not be the case. You are telling them they are always disappointing you and that you can't expect anything more from them.

Ever observed how we play manipulation games and introduce a sense of guilt within our personal relationships a lot of times? Note how the elderly make their children experience a sense of guilt by mentioning how the latter never have enough time for them.

When teens ask for permission from their parents about overnight outings and late party deadlines and are refused, they will go on about how the parents are not letting them live their life or are coming across as too suffocating, overprotective and overbearing. They will talk about how they need to negotiate the world around them sooner or later without their parents being around to protect them all the time.

We all know that one person who is forever blaming other people or circumstances for their shortcomings. They will strategically utilize their sense of helplessness to get the other person to take the desired action. Manipulators give others the impression that they (the other person) have decided their (the manipulator's) fate through their actions and choices, often negatively. Then they will make the victim feel like they are responsible for the manipulator's woes now, and they should make good the damage.

The victims begin accepting this notion that they are responsible for a negative situation created for the manipulator and often respond in the affirmative to the manipulator's request to make it up to the seemingly negative thing they've been led to believe they have done. The manipulator positions himself/herself as someone who needs help and doomed if they don't receive timely help. The other person feels terrible and ends up doing as you want them to because to some extent they feel responsible for your helplessness or unfortunate situation.

4. Play the victim. Where emotional manipulation is concerned, nothing that happens is ever your mistake. Irrespective of your actions, you always blame someone else for their failings.

You harp on how they were made you do something. If they get angry or hurt, you are the one responsible for building unreasonable expectations. If they get angry or upset, you are responsible for hurting them. There is zero accountability for any action.

For example, if a person forgets their partner's birthday, and the partner gets upset about it, they'll generally apologize and promise to make good for it in the future. However, an emotionally manipulative person will not just deny it is their fault; they will also make their partner feel miserable for blaming them.

They will take off about how stressed they've been off late owing to something the partner has done that it's just impossible for them to remember it. The manipulator will go a step ahead and remind you of instances where you've forgotten something important to justify their fault.

5. Emotional manipulators expect too much, way too soon. From an interpersonal relationship to a business association, emotional manipulators are always taking the highway, while overlooking a few steps along the way. They may share too much too early in a relationship and expect the other person to do the same.

Their vulnerability, transparency, and sensitivity are a clever ruse. This is a 'special' charade to make you feel a part of their inner circle. Slowly and insidiously, you'll not just feel sorry about their feelings but also responsible for it.

6. Emotional manipulators belittle your faith in understanding reality. These people, you must hand

it to them, are exceptionally skilled liars and cheats. They will confidently insist something happened when it didn't and deny it happened when it did. They do in such a devious and underhanded manner that you begin questioning your own sanity.

For example, if you suspect your partner of having and confront them about it, the emotionally manipulative partner with outright deny it (even though it is the truth), and in turn make you feel like an insane, suspicious person who doesn't have a grip over reality.

Even though your suspicion is not unfounded, you'll be made to feel guilty about spying around and not trusting your partner. It'll come to a point where you will begin questioning your own suspicious nature and sanity. I am sure many of you are nodding your head in agreement to this!

I know by now you've already identified such people and relationships and chances are weren't even aware of these snarky, insidious tactics when we were being manipulated.

7. Everyone must feel the way they do. Wow, this is another sneaky emotional manipulation technique used to suck other people into their emotional state. The emotional manipulator wants everyone to feel like they are feeling. If they are in a foul mood, everyone around should be aware of it.

However, it doesn't end there. Not only should everyone know how they are feeling, but they should also be sucked into the emotional state of the manipulator. Whatever other people are feeling or experiencing should be dropped down and they should instantly match the emotional frequency of the manipulator. This makes people around them feel like they are responsible for the emotional manipulator's feelings, and they alone should fix it.

8. Eagerness to help becomes a burden later. Emotional manipulators will volunteer to help initially (and pretty eagerly at that) only to make themselves look like martyrs later. They will act like what they initially agreed to do is a huge burden.

If you remind them that they committed to the task, they'll turn around and make you feel like a paranoid person despite them appearing eager to help. The objective? To induce a feeling of guilt, feeling obliged towards them and probably even questioning your sanity!

9. One-upmanship games. Irrespective of the intensity of your problems and challenges, they will always make it come across as their problems are much worse. They will attempt to undermine the authenticity of your problems by constantly reinforcing how bigger their problems or challenges.

They'll make you feel guilt for complaining about 'trivial' things when they are facing serious issues. The goal? You don't have any reason to complain about your 'non-serious', while they have every right to keep reminding you of their 'serious' problems. In other words, they want you to shut up and stop complaining about your problems, and always be one-up in every situation.

10. They know your emotional buttons and how to press them at will. We all have our emotional weak spots. Emotional manipulators are cleverly aware of your weak spots and do not hesitate to use them for serving their own sinister objectives. They will use knowledge of your weak spots against you.

For example, if you are insecure about your appearance, they will pass snide remarks about everything from your clothes to your weight. Again, if you are worried about an upcoming speech, they will prey on your fears by telling you how tough, picky and judgmental the audience is. They use awareness of your emotions not to make you feel better but to manipulate you into feeling worse.

11. Emotional manipulators use humor to take a dig at your perceived weaknesses to disempower you or make you feel inadequate. Notice how some people are perpetually making critical or snide remarks about their partner or friend, often in the garb of

humor. The idea is to make the other person feel inadequate, inferior or insecure.

Emotional manipulators attempt to disempower the person by playing on his/her perceived weaknesses. The remarks encompass everything from the person's appearance to their old phone to their skills. They make sarcastic and seemingly funny comments about everything, including the fact that you walked in 30 seconds late.

The idea is to make you look bad and feel worse about yourself. This way the manipulator tries to gain psychological dominance over you, unfortunately without you even realizing it (now you do, right?). Undermining you makes you perceive yourself as inferior, which automatically gives them the much needed psychological superiority.

12. Emotional manipulators constantly judge and criticize you to make you feel inferior. In the above example, we saw how manipulators use covert techniques to disempower you by disguising their snide remarks as humor. However, here the emotional manipulator outright dismisses, marginalizes, criticizes and ridicules you in a bid to main psychological superiority over you.

Their premise is if they make you feel inadequate and off-balance, their chances of getting you to do whatever they want to increase. You will stop believing in your abilities, sanity, and worth, which will help them wield greater control over your thoughts, emotions and actions.

The emotional aggressor will intentionally foster the feeling that something is not right with you, and that however hard you try, you won't be good enough. Significantly, the emotional manipulator will emphasize the weaknesses without offering constructive or positive solutions or assisting you in meaningful ways to overcome the negatives.

13. Emotional manipulators will give you the silent treatment. Another art emotional manipulators have mastered is the art of giving people the silent treatment to pressurize them into doing what the manipulator wants. They will intentionally make you wait and sow seeds of doubt, insecurity, and uncertainty in your mind. Emotional manipulators use silence as leverage to get you to do what they want by keeping you emotionally deprived or insecure.

Being at the receiving end of the silent treatment is a warning sign you are dealing with an emotional manipulator. It is a type of emotional abuse through which contempt is demonstrated through nonverbal acts such as remaining silent or withdrawing all communication.

The silent treatment is used as a tool to incite their victims into doing something specific or make them feel inadequate by the refusal to acknowledge their presence. If your actions don't match what the manipulator wants you to do, they will utilize the silent treatment for communicating their disappointment and punishing their victims.

14. Pretend play. Yes, they can play dumb too whenever needed. They will pretend that they don't understand what exactly you want or what you desire from them. This is one of the sneaky passive-aggressive tricks, where should be their responsibility, becomes yours. So the onus of what is essentially their responsibility is thrown on your shoulders. This is often used by people who are trying to hide something or avoid an obligation.

15. Raising voice and demonstrating negative emotions. Some emotional manipulators know how to use the power of their voice and body language to coerce you into their demands.

They will often raise their voice as a type of aggressive manipulation with the belief that if they sound intimidating enough with their voice, tone and body language, you will invariably submit to their demands. The aggressor-like voice is often combined with intimating body language such as exaggerated gestures and standing to increase the effect of their aggressive manipulative actions.

16. Negative surprises as a norm. Whoa! Don't these people know how to throw you off balance with their negative surprises in an obvious attempt to gain a psychological advantage over you? They will suddenly come up with some information about not being able to do something or deliver a commitment as promised.

Typically, the negative information is thrown on you without any forewarning to catch you off guard. You are left with no time to come up with a counter move. Emotional manipulators are wolves in sheep's clothing and won't spare a single opportunity to cause discomfort, hurt or harm to you if you get in the way.

Chapter Two: Covert Manipulation Techniques

Recognizing covert manipulation tactics is tricky because unlike overt manipulation these aren't obvious or in your face. They are often underhanded techniques of trying to gain control of the victim's thoughts, feelings, and decisions. It is aimed at bringing down a person's sense of self-worth and destroying their belief in their perceptions. When you learn the manipulator's game, you can play it better than them.

Manipulation undermines the victim's ability to make conscious decisions and act in accordance with their interests. Instead, they become mere puppets in someone else's hands. Manipulators don't value people's personal values, desires, and boundaries. In plain words, they'll make you do something you wouldn't normally do.

So what are the most widely used covert manipulation tactics and how do you spot it in your everyday life? Read on to de-bluff people's covert manipulation games. While these can be used as manipulation strategies by you to get people to do what you want them to, ensure that you do not overuse them or try to lend them as much of a positive twist as possible.

1. Create a false sense of intimacy. Notice how people are constantly sharing intimate information about themselves in the early stages of a relationship? They will talk about their family, backgrounds, and lives (often portraying themselves as victims as circumstances) in a bid to win your sympathy, while also creating an illusion of intimacy.

2. Introduce other people in the picture in a bid to make you insecure. Again, some people are always trying to create a sense of insecurity or discomfort in their victims by introducing other people into the picture. For example, your partner may talk about meeting an ex-girlfriend/boyfriend or good friend to make you feel insecure.

Of course, not everyone who meets friends or ex-partners is being manipulative. However, covert manipulators are constantly using this tactic of introducing other people into the picture to unsettle their partner. When a person is trying to pit other people against you to make you feel inadequate, you can be sure it's a covert manipulation tactic.

3. Another covert manipulation technique is 'foot in the door', which is fairly easy to recognize. It involves making a small request that the victim agrees to, which is subsequently followed by the actually intended request. It is tougher to refuse once the victim says agrees to the initial request.

Foot in the door technique as the name suggests, the objective here is to get your foot in the door until you are comfortably positioned or placed to ask for what you want the other person to do. It can be traced back to the time when door to door salespeople placed their foot in door to prevent prospective buyers from slamming the door on their face. Placing their foot in the door offered them more time to keep the conversation going, and ultimately make a sale. This ingenious manipulation strategy is effectively used across settings even today.

How can the foot in the door manipulation strategy be effectively used in today's scenario?

It is just as simple and efficient, only now you are making headway into a person's mind instead of their door. Start by building a rapport with the person. Attempt to break the ice by making a small request. Remember, the key is to make a small request, which is the other person can easily fulfill. What you are actually doing is slipping your foot in the door to develop a rapport with the person to get them to concede to a bigger or the actual demand later. If you straight away ask for what you actually intend to get them to do for you, they may refuse. Begin with a request that isn't too challenging to meet for the other person. Go for the kill gradually and steadily. Move to the actual request slowly and subtly.

You are trying to get the person to say a series of 'yes' in a sequence before moving in to the actual kill. This will psychologically reduce the chances of the person breaking the pattern and saying no for the final or actual request. This is precisely why psychologists and behavioral experts urge salespersons to ask their prospects several questions that result in a 'yes'. According to research in the field of psychology and behavioral science, if a prospect answers in the affirmative to six questions in a sequence, there are higher chances of them purchasing your product/service or taking the desired action.

Use this information to your advantage by asking people six questions in a series, where they are likelier to reply in the affirmative. The strategy works at a subconscious level and is worth trying.

We launch a sequence of positive replies that make it almost impossible for the other person's subconscious mind to refuse our final request. Once a person starts a loop of responding to your requests in a positive manner, subconsciously it becomes tough to break the pattern, and suddenly offer a negative response.

This is exactly what salespersons in the earlier times did. They placed their foot in the door and offered themselves extra 3-4 minutes with prospects to build the sales pitch momentum, develop rapport and make a sale. Now let's think about the same strategy in today's setting. How do you give yourself that tiny opening that you can eventually cash upon by getting people to do what you desire?

Let us take an example to understand how this manipulation or persuasion can be applied in today's scenario. Jane is finishing the project that requires her to build a model of the nine planets. She asks her mom to help out by creating a rough model for the nine planets project. Of course, her mother does the rough sketch, collects all the required materials to build the model, and keeps everything ready for Jane to make her project. Jane then goes on to request her mom to put all the various pieces together. She does as requested. Finally, Jane's mom finishes doing the entire assignment with no inputs or effort from Jane. Jane used the foot in the door strategy to manipulate her mother into completing her project for her instead of directly asking her to do in the beginning. If Jane would've directly requested her mother to complete the project, she would've refused point blank. However, she got her mom to say a series of 'yes' with small requests that eventually ended with her mother completing the entire project.

This manipulation and persuasion technique for first studied by Fraser and Freeman during the 20th century! The goal is to get people to respond or agree to a tiny and simple request leading to a bigger 'yes.' The psychologist duo realized that once people agree to a seemingly tiny request, the chances of them responding in an affirmative to bigger requests increase. In this example, Jane got her mom to finish the entire assignment by placing together several pieces of the task and getting her to agree to each of these smaller tasks or requests. Once the initial tiny request of creating a rough sketch for the model was agreed upon, Jane could manage to get her mother to meet her larger request. This wouldn't have been the case had she requested her mother to complete the entire project at the outset.

While utilizing the foot in the door strategy, make sure the request is tiny enough for people to not reply in the negative. At the same time, it should be sufficiently important to give the other person the feeling that they have done a good deed by responding to your request in a positive manner. Keep the request positive so other people do not think isn't worth their while to fulfill it. Ensure the request is something that a person will be willing to do without many external influences like rewards or pressure.

If someone refuses the actual request, they'll come across as someone who agrees to something they don't intend to do. When they object to the real request, you will quickly turn the tables to come across as the aggrieved party. It stops being about your demands since you are now the injured ones.

The focus shifts to your complaints and they are placed on the defensive now. Sometimes, warnings and worry about their well being is cleverly hidden as a concern. Manipulators are forever trying to undermine the other person's choices and decisions in an attempt to shake their self-confidence or sense of self-worth. Again, this manipulation technique must be used with sufficient caution and care.

4. "Snakes in Suits" – In their publication *Snakes in Suits,* Robert Hare and Paul Babaik advise how people should guard against manipulators who offer out of place and excessive compliments. It is a huge manipulation red flag. Focus keenly on what's next. Keep questioning yourself, what exactly does this person want from me?

5. Force Teaming. Have you noticed how some people are always creating a forced sense of team spirit or shared purpose where none exists? Typical phrases used by them include, we're one team", "how do we handle this as a team", "we've done it now" etc. They purportedly try to portray that you both are involved in something as a team.

In such a situation, how can you tell if the person is being genuinely helpful or simply trying to manipulate you? Do feel a strange sense of discomfort while accepting their help? Are their words congruent with their body language? (more on body language later) Is the person giving you an option to refuse help? Are they taking your refusal in the right spirit? If no, you may be dealing with a covert manipulator, who is trying to manipulate you under the guise of offering you help.

6. Flattering First Impression. Practiced manipulators often make a stellar first impression. They use a bunch of enticing characteristics such as flawless manners, attractive looks, charismatic smile and courtesy to throw their victims off guard about their real intentions. Yes, they exist beyond the movies, where con men and women are shown to be these stereotypical characters with a dazzling personality and a glib tongue.

With manipulators, what appears on the surface is not the truth. However, with time and observation, you will notice the cracks in their cleverly worn masks. When it gets really sadistic, the silence is used to torture their victims. For instance, a co-worker talks to everyone at work but ignores you or refuses to have any conversation with you.

7. Covert manipulators will appear to be selfless by keeping their real intentions, ambitions, goals, and agendas cleverly cloaked. Their true intentions are hidden under the garb of a selfless cause. This one's tricky to indentify. These are the people who will act like they are working hard on behalf of another person while hiding their true ambition for power and dominance over others.

For example, a covert manipulator will give his/her manager the impression that they are willing to put in extra hours of work when the manager is away on vacation only to fulfill their ambition of eventually taking over the manager's position.

8. Gas lighting. The term gas lighting as a covert manipulation technique comes from the play of the same name which was later adapted into films. It has also been used in literature and psychological research.

Using the gas lighting technique, a manipulator will twist reality to fulfill their objectives. Irrespective of the truth, they have tricks up their sleeves for making you think that it is indeed your fault for not being able to perceive things correctly. It is so deeply ingrained into your mind that you stop trusting your perceptions and instead accept the manipulator's contrived version of the truth. The technique is intended to make you feel so mentally incompetent that you stop trusting your version of reality. It gets to a point where if someone tries to challenge your perceptions, you are mistrustful of them.

9. Rationalization. Rationalization is a technique through which a manipulator offers some form of justification for a hurtful, offensive or inappropriate action. What makes the technique so tough to spot is that the explanation given often enough sense for any reasonable individual to buy it.

Rationalization fulfills three fundamental purposes including, eliminating resistance manipulators may have about their inappropriate action, keeping others from pointing fingers at them and helping the manipulator justify his/her actions in the victim's eyes.

Manipulators who use rationalization will typically behave very affectionately at times and then suddenly act distant or cold. When the victim gets tired of their behavior and confronts them or avoids them, they will most likely scream or cry and mention how they have been depressed or upset off late and how you are such a bad person for confronting them about their seemingly inappropriate behavior when you are one who is behaving insensitively.

They will move you to tears with how stressful their life is, even apologize for it at times. However, within the next few days, they'll repeat the pattern. Manipulators are remarkable performers. They can play the victim's role with ease. They can fake emotions, cry at will, laugh when they want to and pretend to be sad or happy on demand. Carefully examine the acts of people who 'love you' or forever try to gain sympathy.

10. Nitpicking and goal post moving. The difference between positive criticism and negative/destructive criticism is a manipulator will come up with near impractical standards and personal attacks. These

self-proclaimed critics pretend to help your development, when in fact, they don't want to see you improve. They are simply operating with the intention of nitpicking on you, pulling you down and making you a scapegoat in every possible manner.

Covert manipulators are masters in the art of 'moving goalposts' to ensure they are never short of reasons to be disappointed with you. Even when you present evidence to validate your stand or act to fulfill their request, they will come up with another lofty expectation for you to meet or ask for more proof to validate your argument. Yes, who said dealing with manipulators was easy?

For example, they may start by picking on you for not having a successful career. When you have a successful career, they'll question you for not being a multi-millionaire yet. When that expectation is met, they'll demand why your personal-work life is never balanced. The goal posts will keep changing and the expectations will rise higher in a bid to make you feel incompetent in some way or the other.

One of the easiest ways to spot a manipulator is to observe if they are constantly instilling a sense of unworthiness in you or forever making you feel whatever you do is never good enough. A genuine or constructive will never induce a sense of unworthiness in you. They will gently point your limitations and often suggest ways to overcome it.

Manipulators, on the other hand, will never offer suggestions to help you overcome your limitations.

If a person is constantly criticizing you without helping you overcome the issue or limitations in a meaningful way, you may most likely be a victim of covert manipulation. They will cleverly present it as constructive criticism even if it just nitpicking without offering solutions.

If a person keeps demanding more proof for validating your argument or keeps raising their expectations, their aim is obviously not to understand you better. They are attempting to provoke you into experiencing a sense of inadequacy or that you have to keep proving yourself all the time.

11. Withholding apology. Covert manipulators will seldom apologize for their actions. Instead, they will deny, lie or shift the blame to avoid accepting responsibility for their act. Be mindful of this covert manipulation technique by examining if the person apologizes and accepts responsibility for their mistakes.

If a person constantly makes you feel like you are blowing things out of proportion or over reacting rather than apologizing, you are most probably dealing with a covert manipulator. Manipulators have a strong urge to be right even at the cost of mending a relationship. Withholding apology is just another controlling mechanism for them.

12. Undermining your success. I once had a friend who was constantly made to feel guilty about being successful by his partner. He was creating a promising future for them and their future kids, but she constantly made him feel terrible about the fact that he worked so hard and barely had time for her. She accused him of being selfish and thinking only about his goals when it fact, he was building a future for their family.

When you tell your partner or a close friend about a promotion or a new job offer how should they usually react? They should be delighted you are progressing in life. Those who truly care about you will want to see you succeed. Manipulators will constantly try to underplay and undermine your success. They will always find some way to instill negativity in any form related to your success story. This arises from a clear sense of insecurity that you are now becoming more self-sufficient, and will no longer need them.

The feeling that the more successful you become, the less they'll be able to control you leads them to behave in an irrational manner. Thus, they'll make you feel miserable about your success. Sometimes, they'll even get angry for no apparent reason. One of their biggest concerns is that financial independence will give you the ability to survive without their help.

This prospect can be threatening for a person who is accustomed to having his/her friend or partner depend on him/her excessively.

13. Fear-Relief Cycle or using fear followed by relief. This is yet another covert manipulation strategy that is utilized in a variety of settings, popularly used by advertisers, brand managers, and marketers to persuade their target consumer group into taking the desired action in favor of their products or services. How does the fear and relief chain work? It essentially acts on a psychological level that makes the entire process effective.

This covert manipulation technique comprises playing on the other person's fears to get them to take the required action in your favor. You introduce a sense of fear and get them to think of the worst that can happen in a particular situation. This is quickly followed up by offering a sense of relief. The person will experience a huge sense of relief and positivity that helps them make a fast decision to meet your agenda.

Let us look at an example. You begin by saying something like, "When I wore your earrings at the party the other night, I heard a snapping sound. I was sure the earring broke. Later, I realized that my sister was actually watching a video on her tablet. Isn't that funny? That reminds me, can I borrow those beautiful earrings again for an upcoming event?

What did you just do? You took the person through a curve of fear followed by relief to bring about a quick change in their emotions at the psychological level to help them take action in the desired direction. The other person feels a huge sense of relief that nothing actually happened to their earrings and they are in a proper condition. They slip into a more receptive, flexible and positive state of mind, which makes it simpler for you to get him/her to do what you desire.

Start by sowing seeds of insecurity and fear in the other person. Make them imagine the worst that can happen within the given situation. Then, tactfully follow this up by providing a solution or diving into a narrative about how things were not as bad as the other person thought or imagined. Once the person realizes that things are indeed not as unfortunate as they had imagined, it will become easier to get them in a more receptive and agreeable frame of mind. The quick whirlwind of roller coaster like emotions makes it easier for the other person to get into a more positive frame of mind once some hope is offered to combat their fear. This positivity can be used to get them to do what you want them to.

Think about how it impacts the person at a psychological level. The victim goes through a cycle or pattern of powerful emotions. Fear is a huge emotion that is capable of getting people to take a lot of quick actions. However, it should be used sparingly. Beyond a point, if people realize that you simply use fear as a tool to manipulate them, they will stop responding to it. Fear makes people uncomfortable and nervous. This is then immediately followed by positivity, a huge sense of relief and instant hope.

Let us look at another example to understand how a consumerist driven market use this manipulation strategy to the hilt when it comes to getting people to make purchase related decisions. Almost every insurance salesperson uses the fear-relief cycle on his/her prospects to get them to buy insurance from him/her. They will introduce a sense of fear, stress panic and anxiety to the inform prospects about how their valuables are always at a risk of getting lost or destroyed under several unfortunate circumstances. They will talk about thefts, fire, robbery and other unfortunate situations where your precious things can get lost, destroyed or stolen. This will be followed up by bringing in a solution – buy an insurance policy so you don't suffer any financial losses. This fear-relief cycle technique brings in some measure of hopefulness, surety, security, and relief within a person to lead them into making a fast buying decision. They think of the policy as the solution or ray of hope when it comes to protecting the worth of their valuables.

14. Ask Big and Scale Back. This is the opposite of the foot in the door technique. In psychological jargon, this is also referred to as the "door in the face" technique. It starts off by making a ridiculously unreasonable request from someone (which they are guaranteed to reject). Later, you return and ask for something much more feasible and less ridiculous (what you were after in the first place).

It may sound insane, but the idea is to make the other person feel sorry about refusing your initial request (even though it was obviously ridiculous). The next time you come up with something more reasonable, the person will feel obliged to comply. This is like the payback for refusing your earlier request, and they feel more bound to help you than another person. Several companies and salespeople use this technique to sell to their customers.

15 Fake confidence. Alright, so you dress up attractively, sport a sharply groomed appearance, carry the most stylish accessories, and still wonder why people don't listen to you, follow you or subscribe o your views.

Chances are, you are missing the most vital accessory – confidence. Yes, you have to slay the demon of low confidence if you really want to inspire the faith of others. The clothes, accessories, and grooming can only carry you up to a point.

One of the most fundamental principles of confidence is that you can totally fake it even when you don't feel it. It is all about your body language, voice, expressions, and gestures (which are fortunately in your control). You can pretend to be a highly confident persona even when you're feeling like a lemon from within.

Our body language invariably impacts our mental state and vice versa. When you act confident for a long time, you end up confusing the brain into believing that you are indeed a very confident person. The brain then automatically reprograms itself and directs the body to be confident, thinking it goofed up somewhere. So, what starts off as a pretentious act actually leads to you transforming into a more confident and self-assured individual.

You have to act all self-assured and confident if you truly want the other person to buy what you are saying. If you don't look convinced about something, there's a slim chance you are going to be able to convince other people about it. Therefore confidence is one of the most vital accessories for a manipulator.

Chapter Three: NLP Manipulation Techniques

What is Neuro Linguistic Programming?

Neuro Linguistic Programming or NLP in simplest terms is the programming language of your mind. We've all had instances where we attempted to communicate with someone who doesn't speak our language. The outcome? They didn't understand us!

You go to a restaurant aboard and ask for a fancy steak but end up receiving insipid stew owing to the misinterpretation of language and codes.

This is precisely what happens when we try to communicate with our subconscious mind. We think we are commanding it to give us happier relationships, more money, a better job, and other similar things. However, if that's not what is actually showing up, something is being lost in translation. The subconscious/unconscious mind has the power to help us accomplish our goals only if we program it using codes it recognizes and understands.

If you are asking your unconscious mind for steak and receiving stew, it is time to speak its language. Think of NLP as a user manual for the brain. When people master NLP, they become fluent in the language of the subconscious mind, which is excellent when it comes to re-programming their and other people's thoughts, ideas, and beliefs. This gives them the power to influence and persuade people, and on the downside even manipulate them.

Neuro Linguistic Programming is a set of techniques, methods, and tools for enhancing communication with deeper layers of our brain. It is an approach that combines personal development, psychotherapy, and communication. Its creators (John Grinder and Richard Bandler) claim that there is a strong link between language, behavior patterns and neurological processes, which can be used for enhancing learning and personal development.

Influence versus Manipulation

So, do you believe a hammer is a tool of utility or destruction? Well, depends on how you use it right? Or what purpose you use it for?

NLP is potent when it comes to getting people to do what you want them to. It is the hammer that can be used to fix a nail in the wall or destroy a piece of wood. Similarly, NLP can be used to build something positive or it can be used for a destructive purpose (manipulation).

NLP and Manipulation have nearly the same meaning. Both are about generating the desired effect on other people without obvious exertion. However, one key difference between influence and manipulation is that the latter is meant to influence others to meet the manipulator's selfish goals through means that can be unfair, unlawful, sneaky, or insidious. Things are contrived through underhand methods to turn out in favor of the manipulator. A manipulator often preys on the insecurities, fears, and guilt of other people. In turn, victims of manipulation feed dissatisfied, frustrated, trapped and unhappy.

Conversely, influence is the ability to inspire people in an admirable, charismatic and honorable way. We are often inspired by influential people and aspire to model our life on theirs. There is a general feeling of positivity related to them, and we feel positively impacted in their company. Not every influence is positive, which is why we do use terms such as "bad influence" to signify a person's negative effect on us. However, manipulation is never categorized as good or bad. It always operates with sinister motives. That is the primary difference between influence and manipulation.

Influence is a double edged sword that can be used positively and negatively, while manipulation only operates with a negative, narrow and selfish perspective to meet the objectives of the manipulator.

While manipulation has self-centered and questionable motives, influence can also be positive. In contrast to manipulation, influence has positive connotations, which considers other people's needs, goals and desires. Don't we as parents want to influence our children to lead happier and healthier lives? Similarly, as a manager, we want to influence our team to put in their best efforts.

Just like the hammer discussed above, people can use NLP for positively or negatively influencing people to meet their own selfish objectives (manipulation). NLP is a mind control tool that can do both – build and damage. The techniques mentioned here can be used to spot NLPers manipulating you or for you to manipulate other people. Again – you have a powerful tool in your possession that can either be used constructively or destructively.

How is NLP Used For Manipulating People?

NLP training is conducted in a pyramid-like structure, with sophisticated techniques reserved for high-end seminars. It is a complex subject (whoever said anything related to the human mind would ever be easy). However, to simplify a complicated concept, NLPers or people who practice NLP pay keen attention to people they work with. They watch everything from eye movements to skin flushes to pupil dilation to determine what type of information people are processing.

Through observation, NLPers can tell which side of the brain is dominant in a person. Similarly, they can tell what sense is the most active within the person's brain. The eye movements can determine how their brain stores and uses information. It is also easy to decipher whether the person is stating facts (telling the truth) or making up facts (lying) by looking at his/her eye movements.

After gathering this invaluable information, NLP manipulator will subtly mirror and mimic their victims (including speech, body language, mannerisms, verbal linguistic patterns and more) to give a feeling of being "one among them."

NLPers will fake social clues to lead their victims into dropping their guard and entering a more open, receptive and suggestible state of mind, where they become ready to absorb whatever information their mind is fed with. Manipulators will cleverly use language that focuses on a person's predominant senses.

For example, if a person is focused on his/her visual sense, the NLP manipulator will most likely use it to his/her advantage optimally by saying something like, "Do you see where I am coming from?", "Can you see what I am trying to tell you?" or "See it this way?" Similarly, if a person is a predominantly auditory person, the manipulator will speak to them using auditory metaphors like, "just hear me out once Tim" or "I hear you."

By mirroring their victim's body language and verbal linguistic patterns, NLP experts or NLPer manipulators attempt to accomplish a clear objective – building rapport. As discussed earlier, manipulators also try to accomplish this by sharing too much too soon or building early intimacy. The objective is the same – to strike a rapport with their victims, which then makes it easy for the victims to let down their guard.

Once the manipulator uses NLP to build rapport and let down the victim's guard through clever use of body language and verbal patterns, the victim becomes more open and suggestible. Fake social cues are fed to the victim to make their minds more malleable.

Once they build a rapport, NLPers will begin to lead the victim into increased interaction in a sublime manner. After having mirrored the victim and establishing in the victim's subconscious mind that they (the manipulator) is one among them (the victim), the manipulator increases his/her chances of getting the victim to do whatever the manipulator wants. They will subtly change their behavior and language to influence their victim's actions.

The techniques can include leading questions, sublime language patterns and a host of other NLP techniques to maneuver the person's mind wherever as they want. The victim, on the other hand, often doesn't realize what is happening. In their view, everything is occurring naturally/organically or according to their consent.

Of course, manipulators (however skilled) may not be able to use NLP to get people to behave in a manner that is completely out of character. However, it can be used to steer people's responses in the desired direction. For instance, you can't convince a fundamentally ethical and truthful person to act in a dishonest manner. However, you can use it to get a person to think in a specific direction or line of thought. Manipulators use NLP to engineer specific responses from a person.

NLP attempts to accomplish two ends, eliciting and anchoring. Eliciting occurs when NLPers use language and leading to draw their victims into an emotional state. Once the desires state is accomplished, the NLPer will then anchor the emotion with a specific physical clue- for example, tapping on their shoulder. This simply means that an NLPer can invoke the same emotion in you by tapping your shoulder.

For example, let us say the NLP manipulator makes you feel depressed or unworthy using language, leading and other NLP techniques. This is followed by tapping the back of your palms in a specific manner to create anchoring. Thus each time they want to create an emotion of being disillusioned, depressed and unworthiness in you, they will tap the back of your palm. It is nothing but conditioning you to feel in a certain way with linked physical clues.

Now that you have a fair idea of what NLP is or how manipulators can use it for submission, what can you do to guard yourself against NLP manipulators?

Here are some tips to prevent NLPers from pulling their remarkably smart yet sneaky tricks on you.

1. Be wary of people mirroring your body language. Agreed, you didn't know this until now but people imitating or copying your body language is one of the biggest red signals of them trying to manipulate, influence or persuade you to act in a desired manner. I really enjoy testing these NLP experts using subtle hand gestures and leg movements to gauge if they are indeed mirroring my body language to establish a rapport.

If they follow suit, that's my clue to flee! Experienced NLPers have mastered the art of subtle mirroring, which means you may not even realize they are imitating your actions. NLP beginners will instantly imitate the exact same movement in their eagerness to establish a feeling of oneness which is a good way for you to call out their bluff!

If you are looking for a way to manipulate people, mirroring can work wonders "Imitation is the best form of flattery." To make someone take to you instantly, be one of them or better just like them. Mirroring someone's words and behavior is a primordial instinct. It quickly makes people think that you are part of the "clan".

Have you seen how clever salesmen often repeat the words you do or imitate your gestures just to gently persuade you to buy from them? Or how influencers speak "the language of their people" just to win the trust/confidence of their followers. They are doing nothing but using the highly potent mirroring technique.

When you really want to influence people or get them to do what you want, closely observe their behavior, voice tone and pitch, mannerisms, body language, and speech patterns. Then, use the same in your interactions with them to make yourself instantly likeable. Works like magic!

Research has pointed to the direction that people who are mimicked are likelier to respond more positively to folks who mimic them. The way this works on a psychological level is that imitating someone's behavior pattern or words makes them feel a sense of validation. This positivity directly transmits to the person who validated them by mirroring their behavior. They come to associate people who mirror them as positive and likeable. Doesn't your self-esteem and confidence automatically rise when someone emulates you? And you invariably end up liking people who look up to you.

Another potent tip along the same lines is to paraphrase what people say and repeat it, which is also termed as reflective listening. This shows the other person that you've been listening to them, which sort of validates everything they said. Therapists and counselors generously use reflective listening (which is why people love to talk to them).

This technique can be applicable just about anywhere from your employees to your friends to your partner. When you listen to people intently and rephrase what they said as a question just to confirm that you are on the same page, you're making them feel more comfortable about interacting with you. They are likelier to develop positive feelings for you and listen to you more keenly because you've already demonstrated that what they say is important to you.

2. Confuse with eye movements. Another fantastic way to call an NLP manipulator's bluff is to notice if they are playing very close to your eyes or eye movements. NLP users often examine their target or

victim's very carefully. The eye movements are scrutinized to gauge how you access and store information.

In effect, they want to determine what parts of the brain you are utilizing to gather clues about your thoughts and feelings. I say beat this by darting your eyes all around the place randomly. Move it upwards and downwards or from side to side in no clear pattern. You are throwing your NLP manipulator off the course. Make it appear natural. Their calibration will go down the wayside.

3. Beware of people's touch. Like we discussed earlier, one of the techniques NLPers use is anchoring. If you know a person practices NLP and you are in an especially heightened or intense emotional condition, do not allow them to touch you in any manner. Just throw them off the course by suddenly laughing hard or flying in a fit of rage. Basically, you are confusing them about the emotion they need to anchor. Even if they attempt to establish a physical clue to invoke certain emotions, they'll be left with a mixed bag of crazy laughter, rage and whatever else you did.

4. Watch out for permissive language. The typical language used by NLPers include "be relaxed", "relax and enjoy this" and other similar statements. Beware of this NLP hypnotist style language that induces you into a state of deep relaxation or trace to get you to

think or act in a specific manner. Skilled or covert manipulators rarely command in a straightforward manner.

They will cleverly seek your permission to give you the impression that you are doing what they want you to do out of your own free will (one of their many sinister tricks). If you observe experienced hypnotists, they will never outright command you to do anything but seek your permission to make it appear as it is being done organically, with your consent.

5. Guard Against Gibberish

Watch out for mumbo jumbo that just doesn't make any logical sense or twisted/complicated statements that mean little. For example, "As you free the feeling the of being held by your thoughts you will find yourself in alignment with the voice of your success. Does this make any sense? NLP manipulators won't say anything purposeful but rather program your emotional state to lead it where they want to.

One of the best ways to guard against this sort of hypnotism-NLP induced manipulation is to urge the manipulator to be more specific. Can you be clearer about this? Can you specific exactly what you meant by that? It won't just interrupt their cleverly set technique but also force the interaction into precise language, thus breaking the trance brought about through ambiguous words and phrases.

6. Don't quickly agree to anything. If you find yourself being compelled to make an instant decision about something important ad it feels like you are steered in a specific direction, escape the situation. Wait until a day to make a decision. Do not be swept or led into making a decision that you do not want to make on an impulse. Sales professionals are adept at manipulating buyers into purchasing something they don't oneed using sneaky manipulation and NLP tactics. When someone rushes you into a decision, it should be a warning signal to back off and hold on until you've thought more about the situation.

Chapter Four: Persuading and Influencing People

Gratitude is another huge influencer/influencer/role model quality. Efficient manipulators and influencers know the power of simple appreciation for channelizing people in the right direction. A simple gesture like thanking people, appreciating the effort they put into a project or publically praising their skills goes a long way in inspiring their loyalty towards you.

Always chose to recognize the work or efforts of others and focus on lifting them as glowing role models for others. Few things boost a person's morale than being presented as a sparkling example. This not just makes the person feel wonderful but also helps you reinforce what's the right thing to do. Everyone wants to be appreciated and valued, and will, therefore, be motivated to do things as they should be done. Once a person realizes that you are thankful for something, they will keep doing even more of it.

Another tip that can make you a superb manipulator, influencer and persuader is the ability to help people save face in a potentially embarrassing or awkward situation. The person will feel indebted to you for life. They will feel a deep sense of gratitude that you helped them out of a tricky situation, which in turn inspires unwavering loyalty.

You can help deflect focus from the person's blunder. For instance, if someone says something they shouldn't have said erroneously or accidently, quickly change the topic before anyone notices or pretend nothing huge happened.

As an influencer or manipulator, you are showing people that you care enough for them to cover up for small embarrassments or misdemeanours. However, don't let people take advantage of your niceness. Ensure that the person is assertively informed in private (if it's a potentially huge deal) that you won't show similar lenience if it is a habitual offence.

Coach and mentor people instead of humiliating them. If you spot a sincere effort to change, help them change. Work together on strategies that can help them achieve their goals.

Be Relaxed

Relaxed, rational headed and steady demeanours are likelier to achieve success influencing people than emotional, volatile and demanding approach. Being level headed and unperturbed can win you more followers than an irrationally dogmatic attitude.

People tend to listen to you more effectively when you speak slowly in a calm, relaxed and self-assured manner. Launch into an angry rant of name-calling, and you're sure to lose respect over a period of time. Influencers seldom display extreme emotional reactions. They exude natural self-assuredness that ultimately helps them to influencer others about their ideas.

If you truly want people to listen to you, avoid issuing orders. It makes you come across as grossly high-handed and disrespectful. On the other hand, when you demonstrate that you truly care for others' inputs, people are likelier to respond to your request. They will feel belittled and do the exact opposite of what you ask them to.

Instead, make polite and respectful requests. Use the word "please" wherever you can. Instead of ordering a person to go on an outdoor sales call for the day, you can say something like, "Isn't it a lovely day outside today? Wouldn't it be a good day to do your outdoor sales call? Slim chance the person will refuse. Request in a manner that people find tough to refuse.

Be Mindful of Your Body Language

Did you know that body language accounts for 55 percent of the communication process? And that the tone of your voice adds to about 38 percent of the entire communication? This simply means that non-verbal communication is more important than what you speak or verbal communication.

It isn't reduced to what you say but also how you say it or the manner in which you communicate something. Everything from your gestures to posture to expressions eyes impact the message you are trying to convey. For example, when a person has a stoic expression on their face and folds their arms across their chest, you know they are speaking to you in an accusatory manner. However, a more calm voice, uncrossed arms and legs, and a generally relaxed body language will make the other person feel more at ease. They are likely to less defensive and more receptive to the message.

Here are some tips for keeping your body language positive. Face a person while speaking to them. Maintain eye contact without staring and making the other person uncomfortable. It is alright to shift your gaze occasionally. Don't fidget or tap your fingers/feet. It may give your friend the impression that you are just not interested n what he or she is saying. One of the best tips to reveal your interest in the other person or what he or she is saying is to lean in the direction of the person. Keep your body language less rigid, and be relaxed or comfortable.

Body language is an integral component of your persona as a manipulator and influencer. Your voice tone, expressions, gestures, walk, posture and several other non verbal clues are a clincher when it comes to getting people to do what you want them to.

Always keep the tone of your voice assertive, firm, determined and low. Studies have revealed that talking to people in soothing and comforting low tones actually makes them more efficient. This is no way implies you shouldn't have a strong, assured and naturally confident voice that shows you mean business. Just do not go around talking in high tones all the time for the sake of asserting your authority if you want people to take you seriously. Always speak slowly and pause for effective to reinforce authority. You will appear less authoritative if you talk fast without peppering your speech with impactful pauses.

An influencer and manipulator's handshake is firm without being intimidating and tight. Your objective should be to assure people rather than establish a status quo with your handshake. Do not resort to a limp handshake by using only the finger tips of your hand. Use the entire hand. You get a single chance to create a powerful first impression, and your handshake can make an instant impact.

Did you know people seize you up and form an opinion about you in the initial 4 seconds of your first interaction with them? Make each second count. A firm handshake conveys confidence, affability, and positivity. It symbolizes the unison of two powers that can come together to create something formidable. Powerful influencers always shake hands in a manner that conveys their strength and control.

Do not use random, distracting or nervous gestures while addressing your group. Use gestures that complement verbal communication. For instance, if you are talking about a job well done or appreciation directed your company's way, use the thumbs-up gesture. These gestures support your speech and create a memorable impression in the minds of followers.

Always maintain a powerful posture. Strong influencers communicate confidence, self-assuredness, and strength very subtly through their posture. Keep your posture outstretched and open to project transparency, confidence, and power. Your head should be straight. Make unwavering eye contact while talking to people. Do not forget to smile.

One of the neatest tricks before presenting an idea (that you want the other person to agree to) is to practice postures in front of a mirror. You will invariably feel more confident and subconsciously convey to your audience that you are totally in control, positive about the organization's future and capable of setting powerful goals. When on stage, try to walk, pause and walk again for greater effect rather than making erratic movements or remaining stationary. Movement depicts energy, enthusiasm, and engagement, which can be highly contagious for followers.

Anxious gestures such as pulling at your shirt collar or lifting your hair indicates a bundle of nervous energy, which does little to assure followers in a crisis. Employees expect influencers to be calm and in control of the situation when they are rattled. If they detect nervousness in your body language, they tend to lose confidence too. Keep your body language calm, cool and collected to re-establish security. This comforts followers and facilitates collaboration.

Develop an impressive communication style

Everyone has their own preferences and communication styles when it comes to conveying their ideas, thoughts, and concepts. If you want to be in a more commanding position or want others to view you as an influencer, develop a unique communication style. What is your main communication medium? Do you emphasize more on verbal or non-verbal communication?

I once had a trainer tell me that she loved the way I used by hands gesticulate while delivering a presentation. It added more impact to the message and made it even more effective. From then on, I started consciously incorporating these power-packed hand gestures in my presentation to add more punch to it, which really worked for me. What is your communication USP? If you are wonderful with words, use it to your advantage. If you have a more expressive or animated face, communicate through expressions.

Find out your own unique communication preferences. I am an eye-roller so I can easily communicate through my eyes if I am not pleased with something. Take stock of your personal strengths, weaknesses and communication styles. You don't always have to tow other people's lines when it comes to communication. Stand in front of a mirror and observe your communication style. Pay attention to your gestures, voice, expressions, tone – how do you come across to the other person? What are the words and phrases you frequently use? Does your communication style encourage people to listen or switch off? Is your language positive or negative?

For example, if someone isn't performing up to your expectations, do you say "you suck at this" or "you have the potential to do much better than this?" Does your language bridge gaps or destroy relationships? Do your words encourage further conversation? Does it inspire your bosses, coworkers or subordinates to come up with ideas? Are you shutting people down by what you speak? All this is important when it comes to communication within the workplace.

People often have one of these three communication styles, which may vary depending on the situation. Some people have more authoritative or dictatorial styles of communication, while others are more submissive. The third is the assertive category, which is what you should aspire for. Dogmatic or dictatorial says, "I am always right. My word is gospel truth." Submissiveness says, "You are always right and I give in to everything you say.

However, assertiveness says, "I believe I am right but that doesn't mean I don't respect your opinion or your right to differ." Assertiveness is respect for yours as well as the other person's point of view. It is standing up for yourself without putting the other person down. It is the perfect middle way between being dogmatic and submissive. Look at the top management personnel of any organization. More often than not, you'll observe they have mastered the art of putting across their point without offending other people. Of course, they are plenty of exceptions too. I've had my share of bosses form hell! However, people who know to talk so others listen to them without getting offended have pretty much mastered the art of business communication.

Identify a solid common ground

When you find people switching off from a conversation or not responding favorably to what you are saying, switch to another topic. Find a common ground between you and the other person to establish a comfort level. People in sales use this communication technique all the time. They are trained in the art of building a rapport with potential customers.

Look for clues until you find some common ground. Engage the person in conversation on the topic for a while until they thaw. Make them comfortable, and then switch to the back to the initial topic. They'll be more receptive and open to what you are saying. We often give up when we realize that the other person isn't responding or reacting favorably to what we are saying. However, powerful communicators are quickly able to find a connection through a common thread and bring the other person to relate to them in a more positive manner.

Say Things At The Right Time

This is one of the most important pointers when it comes to communicating with people in a professional capacity. Sometimes, the issue in communication doesn't arise based on how something is being said; it is simply about when it is said. If you have an issue with someone at work, address it to them directly rather than letting the entire workplace know about it. Similarly, everyone has their bad days and moments. Show more empathy towards people by understanding them. We all get stressed and have our share of unproductive or inefficient days. It is alright to reach out to people and make allowances for them when they are clearly having a bad time.

There shouldn't be any room for drama within a professional set-up. Ensure that you praise people publically when they've done something wonderful, and criticize them personally. I know a social media influencer who is extremely popular and loved within her community because she lavishly praises people publically. She always highlights their positives and publically acknowledges their strength.

However, when something doesn't go as planned or results aren't up to the mark, she'll call her staff inside the cabin and have a one to one with them. No one gets wind of the conversation she shares with her assistants. This makes her aura very positive and inspiring. It goes without saying that people take her word seriously and listen to her.

Similarly, keep your body language powerful and positive while communicating with people. For example, maintain eye contact to show that you are interested in or respect what they are saying. Be more aware and mindful of your body language while communicating with people. Imagine a co-worker is voicing his or her concerns to you and you place your chin on the hand while rolling your eyes periodically while listening to them. What signal are you sending them? That you don't care a lark about what they are saying or that you are thoroughly bored.

Always use language that resonates with your people. If you are dealing with a bunch of interns, avoid using too much technical jargon that they may not understand or identify with. They may identify with a slightly breezier and millennial lingo. Similarly, if you are addressing a bunch of senior management personnel, you may have to resort to a more technical and professional language that resonates with them.

Unnecessary technical jargon can complicate or confuse people. You may not be able to impart information effectively or convey your ideas in an impactful manner. Use language that triggers greater engagement and discussion. The main objective of communication should be to communicate your point of view in a compelling manner not to smart around.

Use the Sandwich Technique

The sandwich technique may not really qualify as a highly manipulative technique. However, it is effective because it helps you get the other person to do what you want by using the diplomacy card. This is one of the most powerful methods when it comes to communicating something tricky and potentially offensive to your partner. The way it works is – you sandwich a potentially negative or offensive statement between a couple of positive statements.

For example, "Listen, Bridget, I adore you a lot and you truly make me happy. However, I am having a tough time with you working round the clock. If you would just cut down on your work, and we could spend a good time together, I'd be really happy. It feels so wonderful when I am with you." See what we did there? We used a potential conflict causing accusation (you don't spend enough time with me because of your work) between two saccharine sweet sounding statements that are guaranteed to melt your partner's heart.

Don't throw a bomb on your partner by hurling accusations on them out of nowhere. Always use signposts or indicators that you are offering a heads-up about something so they are prepared for it rather than being thrown off guard. If you have genuine concerns that you want them to hear, begin the conversation with something like, "I really want to get this off my chest" or "I could do with some reassurance that…" This way your partner realizes that you aren't really accusing him or her but just need some reassurance and hearing.

Practice Active Listening

Again, communication is as much or more about listening than talking. It involves allowing your other half to know that you are 100% attentive and interested in what he or she is speaking.

It can be in the form of several verbal and non-verbal clues including eye contact, acknowledgement of what they are saying, paraphrasing what they said (to demonstrate you've been keenly listening and want to understand them correctly) and much more. Don't look at your phone or the newspaper while your partner is speaking. Let him or her know that you have their complete attention.

Resist the urge to interrupt your partner while he or she is speaking. Be focused, interested and attentive. I knew a friend who used to interrupt to offer his wife advice each time she aired her grievances at work. A lot of men do this, and it isn't really their fault.

They are simply wired to fix everything since primitive times. A woman may simply want to talk her heart out to feel lighter. She may not necessarily be looking for advice, guidance or suggestions. However, the man believes himself to be her knight in shining armor and starts offering immediate fix-it solutions. This can be true for women too at times. Resist the urge to offer solutions, and instead focus on listening to your partner.

After they are done speaking, you can figure out if they are soliciting advice. Don't jump the gun to throw in your two cents while they are still talking. Allow them to finish before offering advice.

Look at your partner while he or she is speaking and respond occasionally with a nod or verbal clues like "u-huh", "I see" and "hmm." Set aside a daily talk time that is reserved only for you and your partner. It can be during breakfast or dinner or just before you go to bed. Respect the other person's need for talking or even staying silent. At times, the person may not want to talk, which is also alright. They may engage in a conversation when they feel more ready or energetic for it.

Even if you disagree with what he or she is saying, hang in for a while. Make honest and open communication your prime goal for a more rewarding and fulfilling relationship.

Pay Attention to the Overall Message

Reflect upon the message your partner conveyed via their words rather than simply catching a few words here and there. Check with them to know if you truly understand their feelings. You can do a check back like, "Honey, what I understand from what you are saying is" or "If I understand this correctly, then I think you are feeling...."

This tells your partner that you care about what they are saying, and are tuned in to their message. You are deeply invested in ensuring that you understand them correctly, and there's no scope for misunderstanding or miscommunication. Again, this helps you empathize with the other partner's perspective.

However much you detest it, meeting and interacting with strangers is an integral and inescapable part of your life. We come across people we know nothing about in our everyday life. The good news is – there are some smart tricks at hand to get strangers to like you immediately.

Here are my favorite tips when it comes to influencing and manipulating strangers.

Use Their Name Multiple Times

Strangers don't really expect you to use their names as soon as they introduce themselves to you or are introduced to you by a third person. Plus, people are naturally wired to adore the sweet sound of their names (narcissism pays). Once you get to know someone's name, use it a few times during the conversation naturally.

Don't overdo it or it'll come across as fake. I always notice when I address customer service representatives with their names a few times during the call, they become even more eager to help. The person invariably feels a sense of connection or friendliness towards you. The icy vibes of being strangers thaw a bit and he/she becomes more familiar when they address you by your name.

Also, when you repeat a person's name more than once, the chances of remembering it increases. This can save you the embarrassment of forgetting names (and permanently burying your chances of being liked by the person).

Smile and Maintain Eye Contact

This one's a no-brainer all the way. Smile a universal expression of linking or opening up to someone. Offer strangers a genuine and warm smile to increase feelings of familiarity. It makes you come across as more approachable, amicable and friendly. Plus, it establishes a more positive tone for future interactions. The tiny act of smiling leads the brain into releasing chemical hormones that make you feel happier as a person. This way, you'll enter into an interaction feeling friendlier, happier and more positive, which invariably makes you more likeable.

Eye contact is a universal expression or signals of confidence, transparency, honestly and genuineness. More than 50 percent of our communication happens visually. Thus looking into a person's eyes gives them an immediately familiarity boost. Want to come across as confident without bordering on creepy? Maintain a healthy 60:40 ratio.

Use the Head Tilt

The head title is a wonderful non-verbal way to communicate your interest in a stranger or to get a stranger to like you. You simply tilt your head on one side or another. This communicates subconsciously to the other person that you aren't a threat to them because you are exposing your carotid artery. It is the primary artery that supplies blood to your brain, and any damage to this artery can lead to instant death or permanent brain damage. By exposing this region of your body, you are signaling to the stranger that neither are they a threat to you nor are you a threat to them. You are non-verbally setting the stage for a non threatening relationship.

Use Empathetic Statements

Empathetic statements help retain the focus on another person, thus making you come across as more likeable. People generally like the focus to be on themselves and not others. They feel wonderful when they are the center of attention. Don't parrot their statements for it may come across as patronizing or condescending. Rephrase what they've said while keeping the focus on them. The standard formula for creating empathetic statements should be, "So, what you feel or are saying is ....."

This immediately makes them the focus of the conversation. Something like, "I understand how you are feeling." The idea is to always have the other person as the focus of your conversation. This basic formula seldom goes wrong when it comes to being liked by strangers.

Ask For Favors

I know this seems amusing and even counterintuitive. I mean if you asked someone for a favor and they did fulfill it, you'd like them, right? However, Ben Franklin noticed that each time he asked co-workers for a favor, they liked him more than when he didn't ask for favors. This can work for strangers too when it comes to breaking the ice and opening up people towards you. "Oh you work for XYZ Company, I was really hoping to get the contact details of the marketing manager for a brand association or tie-up. I'd be really nice if you could help me with their contact details."

When someone does a favor, they feel great about themselves, and if you ask a person for a favor you are helping them feel wonderful about themselves. This goes a long way in increasing your likeability quotient. It makes the person who is doing the favor bigger or focus of attention, which makes them feel good. However, don't overdo when it comes to asking people favors just so they like you more. Asking for too many favors will have people running in the opposite direction. Thus, you are manipulating a person into developing positive feelings about you by asking for favors.

Keep Your Body Language Open and Approachable

Did you know that strangers form an impression about you within the first four seconds of seeing or meeting you? The first four seconds are highly crucial when it comes to forming an impression of unknown people. This means the person will form an opinion about you even before you probably say anything at all! The onus in such cases is on your non-verbal signals or body language. Keep your body language relaxed and open.

Of course, actions speak louder than words. They work on a very subconscious and primordial level. Keep your gestures, posture, expressions, leg movements, etc. more approachable. This can help determine on a subconscious level whether strangers view you as an open and receptive person. Your body language will determine whether a person likes you or not, irrespective of what you say.

Keep your palms and arms open if you want to come across as a more approachable and receptive person. Your legs should be positioned wider, and the torso along with the head should point in the direction of the person you're communicating with. Added points for maintaining eye contact. Gesticulating involves using your hands to add more meaning or expression to your verbal message. For example, say pointing a finger in a bid to emphasize a single word or phrase.

This makes you more likeable to strangers because you come across as someone who is high on energy, expression, and enthusiasm. You come across as a more expressive, animated and articulate person. People respond more positively to people who are animated in their gestures.

Offer Sincere and Specific Compliments

One of my tips for breaking the ice with strangers is to pay them a genuine and specific compliment. It can be a tiny, casual and specific compliment that brightens up their day. I'd go a step further and ask them where they bought the stuff from. It is an amazing way to open up further conversation avenues. For example, you may ask a stranger or a person who you've just been introduced to where they got their lovely bag or wallet from.

To this, they may reply that they bought it from London while vacationing there. Bingo! This gives you the opportunity to talk about their English holiday. Thus, you trigger a happy memory, which makes them like you. Who doesn't love sincere compliments? A pro tip while offering compliments is to keep it specific so it sounds genuine.

Instead of telling someone how wonderful their outfit is, you can say the cut looks superb on them or you love the way the fit of the attire. Similarly, instead of telling someone that he/she is a good speaker, pick out bits and pieces from the conversation that you really enjoyed. Another favorite is, instead of saying, "you are beautiful" or "you have lovely eyes" say something like, "The color of your eyes is beautiful" or "you have a very soulful pair of eyes." Start with a warm smile, maintain eye contact, and then compliment them on their eyes. It works wonders!

Applaud them for the humor they used in the speech or their powerful vocabulary. Making the compliment specific makes you come across as more genuine than a plain flattery person. Compliments are a great way to get into the good books of strangers.

Make People Laugh

For all the communication tips I give people, this one probably tops the list when it comes to breaking the ice with strangers. People will adore you if you make them laugh. It is not secret that salespersons who make their potential customers laugh score high sales figures or customer service representatives who make customers laugh score high on customer satisfaction.

Ensure that you don't crack offensive jokes or resort to humor related to sensitive issues such as religion, rac, etc. Keep it clean, intelligent, simple and healthy.

People are generally stressed, exhausted and bored with their daily grind. When you resort to humor, you lighten up their day by making them laugh. It gives them a break from a mundane existence, which makes you endearing to them. If they tell you they are having a tough day or were late for work today, give it a more light-hearted-spin. This will transform their sullen mood, and make them more receptive to a conversation.

Some of my favorite people in the world are those who make me laugh, and it isn't much different for the majority of people.

Avoid Getting Angry

There was a small boy with a rather foul temper. His dad handed him a bag of nails and asked him to hammer a nail into the fence each time the boy lost his cool. The first day saw 37 nails being drilled into the fence by the boy. Gradually, the number of nails drilled into the fence reduced. The boy discovered he it was easier to just hold back his anger than go through the entire process of drilling nails into the fence.

One day the little boy did not lose his temper even once. He went and told his father proudly. The father then asked him to remove a nail for each day he was successful in holding his temper. Several days passed and the nails were now all gone. The father then held his hand and took him to the fence. He said, "You did it, well son. However, look at the holes left behind. The fence can never be the same again. When you say things in a rage, they leave permanent scars behind. It doesn't matter how many times you feel or say sorry, the wound is forever."

It doesn't pay to be a modern day Adolf Hitler. Harsh reprimands may get people to perform out of fear in the short run. However, it will be least effective in the long run, owing to reduced team morale, low motivation, and a non-existent higher purpose for achieving the goal. Be patient and tolerant of people's weaknesses. Rather than getting angry, see how you can help them overcome these shortcomings to boost productivity.

The famous Machiavellian quote comes to mind. "And here comes the question whether it is better to be loved rather than feared or feared rather than loved." While a balance of both is ideal, love may help you gain fierce loyalty, companionship, and faith. It makes followers intrinsically motivated to put in their best to prevent letting their influencer down. This can be far more potent than physical rewards or reprimand.

You may believe fear is more potent and stable when it comes to getting tasks done. However, it can also lead to corruption and unscrupulous means in which people try to bend the system to avoid reprimand.

Rather than acting with a sense of internal loyalty, they are simply doing things to avoid punishment or the wrath of their influencer, which may lead them to unethical means.

Take Adolf Hitler for instance. He was someone who led by nothing but fear. He rose to power quickly by instilling a sense of fear into his followers. People had little choice but to comply. What were the results? Devastating, to say the least.

Comfort People When They Make Mistakes and Build Trust

Always be a source of comfort for people when you want them to perform and intended action or think in a certain way. People should be able to feel secure and comforted in the bleakest hours. Do not be a source of depression, negativity, misery, and disheartenment of your followers. How do you deal in situations where your spouse, employees, children, and others close to you disappoint you? Do you react immediately and cause even more damage to the already volatile situation? That may not be the best way to deal with the situation.

It helps to comfort people when they make mistakes or disappoint you because this only makes them regret the mistake than get defensive about it. If you launch on an offensive, be ready to accept a truckload of excuses and defenses. Rather than blaming people or accusing them, try to win their confidence by talking sense to them. Manipulators know how to forgive people or overlook their faults and later use this forgiveness as a leverage to build trust to get the other person to take the desired action or think in a certain way.

Let us consider an example. An otherwise brilliant employee Rick has been rather disappointing in his latest project. Instead of belittling him for slacking, try and comfort him to understand what really led to this unlikely situation. Ask Rick if there is something you can do to help him. Try and find out if anything has changed over the past few days or if his morale is low.

Accusing and reprimanding people may not take you too far. You may not reach the root of the problem. Fear doesn't foster constructive talks. Let us assume Rick has made a new bunch of friends, who drink in the local bar until late night everyday, which has led to him not being able to give sufficient time to work. He may not share it with you if he finds your approach condescending and critical. Once you identify the problem, you can work together to resolve it. However, to pin down the problem, you need to be approachable, assuring and comforting influencer.

Discard Grudges and Stay Positive

As a manipulator or influencer, it is critical to set the rhythm for a more inclusive organizational culture that thrives on progress, positivity, and forgiveness over back-biting, vengeance, and loose talk that can hinder productivity. Since influencers operate at the focal point of human relationships, every move of theirs should be directed towards setting an example for large heartedness and forgiveness.

Reflect and remind yourself that holding a grudge or ill feelings against people builds negativity within you and subconsciously helps the other person detect it. It soaks your energy and may lead to irrational or negative actions. It takes away the focus from productive goals. Walk in someone else's shoes. Imagine yourself in their place to try and understand what drove them to behave the way they did without harshly judging their actions. You do not have to endorse or whole heartedly agree with their actions. Try and see where they are coming from. Once you show people some unexpected understanding, they will feel indebted to you. This can be later exploited to get them to take the desired action.

Rather than holding grudges and seeking vengeance, talk to the person honestly about how you felt and get it over with. You will feel better and less prone to housing grudges after expressing yourself. Forgiving and forgetting the act needs closure. Do not speak to people in anger, while also freeing yourself from holding any grudges against them. Also, if doesn't help to simply speak politely to people on the face and hold grudges against them within you. Get rid of all ill feelings internally and externally. Show compassion, speak gently, try and understand what led people to behave the way they did and forgive them inside out.

One of the best strategies for discarding grudges is to come to some sort of understanding with a person or group of people. Get clear assurance that people will not repeat their actions. This will gradually help you re-establish trust and eliminate grudges.

Forgiveness doesn't make you any less of an influencer. It doesn't imply that you are not operating from a power position or surrendering your dominant role. It simply means you are wise enough to let go of negative emotions and focus on positivity for increasing the organization's productivity.

Be positive is the blood group of all influencers. On a more serious note, everyone has some positive and negative characteristics. If you've found the perfect being, you probably exist on another planet. Great influencers, persuaders and manipulators know the value of cultivating a culture that encourages employee errors as a way for learning and growing. Though this sounds overtly optimistic, it leads to fewer errors in the long haul. Every failure can include some learning.

Rather than focusing on your employees' weaknesses, try and highlight their strengths even when referring to their mistakes. This gives a powerful positive twist to the process of evaluating their action. Let us consider an example. An employee Ann lacks time management skills due to which she missed a couple of deadlines. However, she is great with research.

Start by telling her how wonderfully well researched the project is and how much more appreciation it was capable of bagging had it been turned in on time. This doesn't make your team members feel devalued or de-motivated. They will be more driven and determined to learn from their mistake in the future. Simply highlighting the negatives makes the employee's morale hit rock bottom.

One solid tip for gaining people's undying loyalty and allegiance is to be good to them when they least expect it. People automatically assume harsh reactions from influencers when they make mistakes. However, if you treat them gently and compassionately by highlighting their positives, you are only boosting their morale for not repeating the mistake.

Criticize or admonish the mistake not the person. A mature influencer does not resort to name calling and launching personal attacks. People get frustrated and demoralized when you criticize them rather than singling out their acts. It builds resentment and rebellion in followers. People will not be very comfortable openly discussing matters with an influencer who resorts to criticizing them over their acts. When people make mistakes, they are already feeling miserable about it. When you forgive them for it, they will always remember the favor. This gives you a solid foundation to get them to do what you want them to later.

Speaking harshly is like rubbing salt on their existing wounds. Do not say something like "you are such a terrible worker." Instead, try saying "what you did was not the best thing to do. Instead, you could have done this." This way you are still pointing out the mistake without coming across as personally offensive. Also, when errors happen and problems arise due to them, get rid of the blame game. Be a part of the solution instead of making people feel terrible about their mistakes. An effective influencer moves over from the problem and uses a solution oriented approach. Focus on how to remedy the problematic situation.

Chapter Five: Tackling Manipulation in Relationships

Emotional manipulation or being in a manipulative relationship is one of the most unfortunate things a person can experience. Not only does it destroy your sense of self-worth but also prevents you from enjoying fulfilling and rewarding relationships in the future. Manipulation goes against the ethos of a healthy, happy, positive and inspiring relationship.

While we are all in some way or the other manipulating our loved ones, it becomes sinister when it hits at a person's emotions or sense of self-worth for fulfilling a selfish agenda. Here are some effective deals for dealing with manipulation in relationships.

1. Closely observe your feelings after every interaction. Do a majority of your conversations or interactions with your partner make you feel confused, unworthy or overcome by self-doubt? By doing a routine check of your feelings, you will be able to identify a clear cause.

For example, if you realize that you always feel guilty after a conversation with your partner. Rewind to the conversation and go over what your partner said after each interaction. How did it start? What are the typical words and phrases they use while talking to you? Is there a pattern to what they say and how they make you feel?

It would be even better if you can make a note of your feelings to easily identify the emerging pattern.

Tell yourself that the problem is them and not you. Remember that you are only being hoodwinked into thinking it is your fault or you aren't good enough. The manipulator is most likely dealing with grave issues of their own, which they are incapable of handling effectively. This is only to help you establish a context for their acts, not to make you feel sympathetic towards them. Keep in mind, manipulators seldom deserve sympathy!

2. Assess your relationship objectively. If you can't determine if you are truly in a manipulative relationship or the person, get a reality check by talking to friends or people you trust.

Ask them for an objective assessment of your relationship frankly. Do they think your partner has unreasonable expectations from you? Do they think your partner is taking advantage of you? Do they you are being emotionally vulnerable?

Sometimes by talking to a third person, we gain a perspective we hadn't considered before. It'll probably give you a new way of looking at things, which will allow you to act immediately if you are being manipulated.

3. Confront the manipulator. Consider various angles before going for the kill and confronting your manipulator. They most likely won't admit to their manipulative acts, especially if you sound unsure and nervous.

Rather than making blanket statements about how "they have been using you" or "taking advantage of you", get down to specifics. How does a specific action or words make you feel? List specific instances where you felt you were taken advantage of. Follow this up with a positive and gentle yet assertive request to mend their behavior.

You are communicating to the manipulator that you are aware of their tricks, which makes them more cautious while manipulating you. In the same vein, you are also giving them an opportunity to get their act together. It will take real effort and commitment on your part to move out of an emotionally manipulative relationship. You will have to stay vigilant and develop limitless reserves of self-esteem and positivity.

4. Hit hard at the center of their gravity. If nothing else seems to work, hit the manipulator hard on his/her center of gravity. They'll often resort to evil strategies such as befriending your friends and then speaking evil about you or tempting you with a reward and then backing off or not honoring their commitment.

Since you know the person inside out, hit them where it hurts the most. Their center may be their friends, followers or anything they think is integral to their existence. Use this knowledge to beat them in their own game.

5. Don't fit in with their ideas. The key to avoid being manipulated is to reinvent yourself and have your own ideas about things rather than subscribing to theirs. Manipulators will shove their ideas down your throat since they need to control you to further their agenda. Have your own clear views, ideas, and opinions about various aspects of your life. Consistently drilling a particular idea in your mind is how they are able to successfully confine you in a box.

Don't try to fit in, focus on reinvention. Work hard towards standing out from the rest. Be different, unique and remarkable in your own way. Personal growth and building your self esteem is the key for fighting manipulation.

6. Don't compromise. Guilt is a powerful emotion leveraged by manipulators. They will use your self-doubt and guilt to their advantage. The agenda is to knock your sense of balance and instill a sense of uncertainty with you. This uncertainty eventually drives you to compromise on your values, ideals, and goals.

Avoid feeling guilty or compromising. Don't doubt yourself or your abilities. Even though you are in a relationship with a person, you don't owe them anything if you are not treated with respect. Every person deserves to feel wonderful and positive about themselves. If a person doesn't make you feel good about yourself or your accomplishments, there may be a problem. Have a firm belief in your values and ideals. Don't compromise on your values, beliefs, goals, and ideals. Remember, you deserve to feel great about yourself and your achievements. There should be a strong sense of self-belief, self-assuredness, and confidence in what you are doing.

A manipulator becomes powerless in the face of high self-confidence. They start losing their influence once you learn to operate with confidence and refuse to compromise on anything that undermines your self-respect or core values.

7. Don't seek permission. This is like handing the manipulator the pass to manipulate you as they wish. The trouble is, since childhood we've been conditioned to seek permission. As an infant, we seek permission to eat and sleep. All through school we are seeking permission to visit the bathroom, eat our lunch or drink water.

A direct consequence of this is, even as grown-ups, we don't stop seeking permission from people close to us. Instead of informing your partner you are planning to meet a friend over lunch, you'll subconsciously ask them if it is alright if you plan something with your friend. By constantly and habitually seeking permission, you are only giving control of your life to someone else, especially if he/she is a more manipulative type.

Don't be overly concerned about being polite or making others feel good at the cost of your own comfort and happiness. Remember, you have the right to live your life exactly the way you want to. Emotional manipulation is about making you feel beholden or enslaved by some imaginary rule that exists only in the mind of the manipulator. They'll never want you to feel self-sufficient and take your own decisions because that diminishes their hold over you.

There's no need to bow to their authoritative dictates or consult them before everything you do unless it does impact them in an important manner. I happened to have a co-worker who would seek his girlfriend's permission even before going for a coffee break or out for lunch. It was ridiculous the way she treated him and tried to control every move of his. Predictably, the relationship ended on a sour note.

However, no one can make you feel miserable without your permission. And by constantly seeking permission, you are giving your partner permission to make you feel miserable – if that makes sense. You can disregard the manipulator's obsession with confining you anytime by living your life the way you to, without their interference or permission.

8. Be open to new opportunities. The manipulator wants you to put all your eggs in their basket so they can throw away the basket whenever they fancy. Don't lock yourself into them or be tied down by a commitment you aren't comfortable making. Don't be content or accept your current life. If you are in a highly manipulative or emotionally/physically abusive relationship, attempt to break free and explore other relationships or opportunities.

Manipulators in relationships often take advantage of the fact that their partner is "used to them", "addicted to them", "can't do without them" or "can't get anyone better." We often stay in abusive relationships because we believe that we don't deserve any better or won't get anyone better. There is a fear of loneliness or a false sense of being in the cocoon of a relationship.

Break free from such self-limiting and unhealthy thought patterns. Of course, you deserve better in life or will find someone who treats you with respect and dignity. To keep you your place, manipulators will resort to plenty of name calling. If you express a desire, they will make you feel like you are arrogant, selfish, proud, cold, and inhumane and many other uncharitable labels.

They want to keep you dependent on them. By seeking out new opportunities for jobs, relationships, hobbies, etc, you are only weakening their control over you. Seek out new people, make new friends, join a hobby club, volunteer with an NGO. Do something purposeful and meaningful that gives you the opportunity to meet new people and live a more intentional life. This is the only way to start becoming self-sufficient and independent.

9. Don't be a baby. If you are fooled once or twice, you are vulnerable but if you constantly let people walk over you without learning your lessons, you are a downright idiot. Stop letting manipulators take advantage of your gullibility. Develop self-awareness about manipulators and know how they operate. Have enough self-respect to refuse manipulators.

I know a lot of people who sleep walk through life, allow people to take advantage of them and then blame others for their situation. You can't go around oblivious to manipulators trying to use you to fulfill their agenda. Rather than blaming the evil around you, become smart and take control of your life. Yes, the unfortunate truth about life is negative and manipulative people exist. The take advantage of people to further their agenda

However, this shouldn't be your ticket to making the same mistakes again and again and crying foul. Manipulators cannot manipulate without the permission of their victims. Accept responsibility for your success and failure. If you are outsmarted or out strategized, it isn't someone else's fault. Learn from past mistakes. Watch out for a pattern that may reveal your own vulnerabilities. Don't keep trusting the wrong people again and again.

Similarly, don't keep giving a chronically manipulative person multiple chances. Break free from them. Remove manipulators from your life. Commit to the pursuit of surrounding yourself with positive, encouraging and like-minded folks who don't take advantage of you.

Remember, you have complete control over your life. Place your bets on yourself and not other people. If you place your bets on other people or rely excessively on other people for your happiness, you make yourself more vulnerable to manipulation.

Again, manipulation victims are not very confident about their judgments. Learn to trust your judgments and instincts. You know what is good for you much better than anyone else. Don't go around asking people things such as "What am I good at?", "what I do", "who is the real me" etc. You are simply opening the doors of manipulation. Don't go around demonstrating your lack of understanding about yourself.

Again, I know a lot of people who go around seeking constant validation from others. They look at other people to define them. These people won't even buy a pair of trousers if it isn't approved by others. Why should others define you?

Define yourself and trust your judgment. Winners are not people who have a more evolved ability to listen to others. They are the ones who have developed the ability to tune in to their beliefs and judgments. They don't rely on external validation or approval of their beliefs. An established trust in your beliefs and judgments makes manipulators powerless. When you don't seek validation from others, they don't have an upper hand of how they make you think and feel. Start trusting your instinct and judgment!

10. Dependent manipulators. This is a little opposed to the stereotypical image of a manipulator but they exist. Contrary to most manipulators, a dependent manipulator will constantly make you feel like they are powerless and completely dependent on you. They accord you the higher position in a relationship to such as extent that you feel emotionally exhausted while dealing with them.

The way to handle this type of manipulation is to gradually get them to make decisions. Make them realize that they are as much responsible for their well-being as you are. Consciously put them into positions where they are forced to make a decision. Talk to them about how their lack of responsibility to decision making is stressful for you. Over time, they may enjoy taking responsibility.

Chapter Six: Manipulating Mass Opinion as a Public Speaker

If there's one thing that distinguishes influencers from average Joes, with everything else being the same (talent, knowledge, skills), it is the way influencers talk. Influencer talk is no magic language. However, it is everyday language spoken effectively. Influencers know the secrets of impact communication, and hence are able to draw a larger audience. If you've spent some time studying influencers, you'll realize there's something that sets them apart from typical employees. They exude an aura of confidence, an undisputed magnetism, and clarity in communicating their message. Their vocal presence is enough to inspire and encourage the crowds.

From Benjamin Franklin to Bill Clinton, good influencers are exceptional communicators who've mastered the fine art of influencing their audience through their voice and words.

They understand that their charisma lies in talking in a manner which inspires people to listen to them. So, what's "influencer speak," you ask? Here are some proven tips that can get you to talk the talk.

1. Ditch Those Verbal Clutches

People often make fabulous points when addressing a group of people, but ruin everything in an instant or lessen the impact/effectiveness of their points by including throwaway phrases that do not contribute towards making the message more power packed. For instance, people often end sentences with "and other things" "so on and so forth" and "you know things like that." These are nothing but lethargic linguistic slips that happen when you don't know how to end a sentence/argument with impact verbal posture.

These verbal crutches are most prominent when you take a pause while addressing a group or delivering a speech/presentation. The unintelligible sounds like "er", "um" and "aa" can be hugely awkward and ineffectual. So are gestures of lip-licking, dramatic hand movements, and constant coughing. These are all distracting or listeners, and seriously hit your credibility as a speaker. The primary issue is very few of us actually realize there's a problem in the first place.

One of the best ways to tackle this is to use a phone app and record yourself speaking on a random topic extemporaneously for a couple of minutes. Then, go back to the recording and note the number of times you've utilized verbal crutches. This simple technique will help you become less self conscious while speaking.

A good narrative and effective language involves using definitive words delivered with panache and humility. Refrain from using terms such as, "like" and "sort of." It isn't just weak and ineffectual but downright jarring for the audience.

2. Use Superlatives Sparingly

When you drop "awesome", "fantastic", "epic", "incredible" and the likes at every given instance, it starts to lose meaning. Over emphasis on superlatives washes its real meaning. Each time an influencer or role model assigns extraordinariness to commonplace things; he/she contributes towards making them sound repetitive, which means the really exceptional does not stand out.

So each time you're tempted to say that someone's presentation was amazing or the project was "awesomely" handled, take a few minutes to reflect on your choice of adjectives instead. Speak about how the project was well-researched, comprehensive and full of rare data. Generic praises or descriptions don't go a long way in inspiring people or getting them to listen to you. "This is very detailed and articulate" can go longer than "good work" in uplifting people's spirits, while making you come across as an effective communicator.

3. Resist from Pulling Back

Resist trying to equivocate when talking about crucial or tough topics. It is understandable that talking about not so pleasant things requires huge verbal and personal courage, however, there's no point in pulling your punches when important matters have to be conveyed to the team.

Resist the urge to use sluggish language since using clear, concise language will only boost your courage and help you connect/internalize what truly needs to be said, however unpleasant it may seem.

Use concrete and correct phrases to describe the situation. Clarify your stand if needed. As an influencer, you're going to have to learn to call a spade a spade. Practice speaking in front of the mirror if you get the jitters before a big or important presentation or address. You'll notice your gestures, expressions, body language and basically know exactly how effective you appear to an audience to make the required changes.

4. Simplify the Narrative

Use the age-old narrative for structuring your speech – Introduction, Body, and Conclusion. The less complicated your narrative, the easier it is to comprehend. Know exactly what information to include and what to eliminate to keep it brief yet impactful. No one likes to hear someone go over the same ideas repetitively. Ultimately, the thought loses its impact.

As a thumb rule, avoid speaking about more than a slide per minute, and more than four points per slide. If there's more information to be covered while you're addressing a group, talk only about the highlights, while you distribute hand-outs to your audience. Always attempt to open and close the presentation with a similar slide to maintain uniformity and a good symmetry. Use graphics and videos to aid your narrative and tell a good story.

Also, pay close attention to your inflection during the narrative. Too many aspiring influencers and influencers inflect up towards the end of their sentence, producing a highly annoying sing song effect that makes you sound ineffective and timid. Inflecting down makes you sound authoritative and certain, which is vital when it comes to influencing people.

The uptalk or rising inflection talk makes you come across as an individual who lacks discipline, confidence, and mindfulness. Stop right now if you're doing this.

Cliff hangers are another absolute no-no for a charismatic influencer. Many presenters reach a brilliant crescendo in their talks only to kill it all by not knowing how to conclude clearly and resolutely. This is especially true if you are influencing people to buy from you. You need to include a definitive "call to action" or trigger people in the right direction by ending the pitch persuasively. End with the required impact and a leave a few seconds for the audience to digest your closing remarks or questions.

5. Overlook Verbal Lapses

How many times have you observed presenters awkwardly disrupting the momentum of a speech by apologizing for a lapse no one even noticed? It's alright to stumble over a few terms here and there while addressing an audience or group. Unless it's a huge blunder with important ramifications, there's no need to stop midway for apologizing. Keep going as if it wasn't a big deal.

A majority of the folks don't notice these slip-ups until you voluntarily mention it, which draws pointless attention to it and takes the focus away from your main message. It doesn't just disconcert you but also throws the audience off gear.

6. Create Memorable Audience Moments

Most speakers mistakenly believe that the presentation or talk revolves around them. Nothing can be far from the truth. To make your talk more impactful, make it about your audience. They are likelier to listen to you and get influenced when they realize it is centred on them.

Recognize or appreciate an audience member, maybe a stalwart who has been working tirelessly for the organization and is due to retire soon. Hail a significant recent accomplishment by an audience member. The more you draw your audience into the limelight by recognizing their efforts, the greater are your chances of increasing your own recognition powers.

Chapter Seven: Manipulating with Small-Talk

Studies have it that when you meet a person for the first time, they judge you within the first 4 seconds of the interaction. Yes, that is correct. They decide whether they like you or not within 4 seconds of meeting you. Scary? How do you win people you've only just met? I've got a magic potion for that too – it's called small talk.

Though it may seem pointless, small talk is a brilliant ice breaker that pulls down elements of awkwardness and uneasiness between folks. It makes you come across as a friendly and likeable individual, apart from helping you develop a sound rapport with people and create a stellar first impression. Small talk also lays the base for a rewarding and gratifying relationship ahead. It creates a more positive and beneficial atmosphere that can trigger larger conversations.

When it comes to breaking that initial awkward ice and setting the stage of a meaningful/fruitful relationship, few things work as miraculously as small talk. Whether it is a business networking meet or a dating club gathering, small talk goes a big way when it comes to manipulating and influencing people, building relationships and being a charismatic persuader.

Ever wondered how some people consistently manage to get people to buy their drinks at the bar or make friends in hordes wherever they go? Why do interactions with some people remain etched in our memory forever while we can barely recall others? The answer is well, small talk. Here are 15 rules for winning people using the power of small talk.

1. Stick to Safe Topics

When talking to people you've only just met, always stick to universal, harmless and non toxic topics (especially folks from another culture, place, race, religion, etc). Infallible small talk topics include weather, movies, world economy, breaking news, and food. A pro tip suggested by social psychologists is to base your conversation as much as possible on common grounds. Identify the common ground between you and the other person and stick to those subjects.

It is easy to gauge a person's comfort level about a particular topic through their body language (unless they read a ton of self-help books like you and have learnt to fake it). If their reaction to a specific topic is positive and enthusiastic, keep at it. Always watch out for the non-verbal clues when bringing up a new small-talk subject. Manipulators know exactly how to bring the other person in a more positive frame of mind to get them to do exactly what they want them to. Once a person develops a solid rapport with you and feels good in your company, he/she is likelier to do what you want them to.

2. Ask Open-Ended Questions

The golden rule for drawing people into a conversation or getting them to share more in your initial interactions is to ask more open ended questions. Influencers and influencers understand the importance of asking gentle and genuine questions that reveal that they are truly interested in knowing more about the other person.

One of the biggest manipulation strategies when it comes to establishing a rapport with strangers or making small-talk is gathering as much information about them as possible and leveraging this information to get them to take the intended action.

For example, if you've just learnt that the person you are conversing with is part of a local NGO, ask open ended questions related to it. What inspired them to be a part of the NGO? What are the drives that he/she has been a part of?

Learn to notice what people are truly passionate about, and create a conversation flow based on asking open ended questions related to that topic to learn more about them. If someone's innately passionate about exploring different places and culture, ask about their latest vacation. Keep away from controversial and personal topics. The person will quickly take to you if you sound genuinely interested in knowing more about their interests.

3. Go Easy on the Humor

Sometimes people are so eager to make an impression by coming across as witty and humorous that they end up rubbing people the wrong way, especially folks whose tastes you know nothing about.

To avoid humor from backfiring, go easy on jibes, sarcastic remarks or tongue in cheek humor. It may seem funny to you, but the other person may not appreciate it. Even seemingly harmless comments convey the wrong impression about you. Intelligent/smart neutral jokes/comments are alright to a certain extent but don't make it personal.

Avoid trying to appear too clever or familiar by poking fun at folks without understanding if they are capable of taking it in the correct spirit. Take time to know and understand people well without acting all familiar and extra-friendly.

4. Disagree Amicably

To avoid making your initial conversation controversial, express your disagreement without diplomacy. Instead of launching into an acrimonious attack or defensive name- calling (absolute no-no), try a more politically correct (yet genuine) approach.

Say something genuine and non-controversial like, "that's an interestingly different perspective really. I am now curious about that point of view. Can you explain further?" you are stating that the view doesn't match yours without setting the stage for World War 3.

5. Be an Exceptional Listener

It's no secret. In a world where everywhere wants to talk about themselves, good listeners are highly revered. It is easy to influence people when they are convinced that you are genuinely interested in what they have to say.

People erroneously believe that being a good communicator is all about possessing top notch speaking skills. That's only one half of it folks. The other probably more important half is listening.

Being a social skills ninja doesn't mean you talk nineteen to the dozen without giving others an opportunity to speak. Influencers know when you let others speak, and respond in a positive/encouraging manner.

Show people, you are earnestly interested in what they are talking through verbal and non-verbal clues.

Acknowledge or paraphrase what they say so they know you are actually listening to them. Nod, express with your eyes, lean forward and keep your arms/legs unfolded (to show you are open to listening to them) to reveal your interest in what they are talking through non verbal reactions.

Everyone loves affirmation signs that they are being eagerly listened to, which in turn encourages them to reciprocate when you speak. Exceptional influencers, role models and influencers understand the power of developing great listening skills to make themselves more likeable to their followers.

6. Reveal An Interesting Fact About Yourself

Okay, this doesn't mean you launch into a personal overdrive about who you are dating or that your bank account has just clocked a million dollars. However, a fun, harmless and interesting fact about yourself makes you instantly likeable to people. They will be likelier to tune in to what you say when they realize you trust them enough to share things about yourself. Don't make it too personal for comfort though – that's the golden rule.

It can be something along the lines of your favorite author and why you love his/her work. Why you chose a particular vocation or major in college? Why you enjoyed traveling to a particular place and enjoyed its vibe/culture? It should be like an interesting teaser of yourself (why you love cupcakes or why you decided to call your dog by a particular name) without sounding personal, boastful or over the top.

7. Avoid Conversation Dead Ends

There will be those awkward conversation gaps which you may not succeed in filling. The best thing to do in such a scenario is to look around you for clues to revive the conversation. It can be anything from a flyer to other people around you to details about the venue you're at. There are conversation clues almost everywhere that you can start building a stimulating and meaningful conversation on.

8. The Fine Question-Statement Balance

Maintain a fine balance between making statements and asking questions. A successful small talk brilliantly mixes questions and statements brilliantly to create more wholesome sharing.

Too many queries will make it seem like a one way interrogation. While too many statements will make it look like the talk is centered only on you, which can be highly annoying for the other person.

Role models know how to balance the conversation so people listen. Pepper statements with thought questions, such as, "I am really into aerobics and Zumba, how do you spend your leisure hours?" or "I really enjoy watching that reality show though most people think is scripted, do you watch it?

You're sharing your views but you are also giving the other person an opportunity to share his/her opinion. This back and forth technique gives you a nice, well-rounded conversation.

9. Empathize With People

Empathizing with people is one of the most sure-fire ways of winning their trust and getting them to like you. Don't confuse empathy with sympathy. Empathy is not about feeling sorry for someone or making them feel pitiable about themselves. It is about placing yourself in someone else's shoes and trying to understand how they feel or the emotions they go through.

Saying things like, "I really understand why you feel the way you do" or "I truly understand how you feel about this topic" or "it must've been so tough for you but you've shown exemplary courage" goes a long way in building rapport with people. This sets the foundation for an equation based on empathy, comfort, and understanding, which is what influencers/role models need to inspire in their followers.

People are likelier to talk and share their feelings with you when they realize you understand where they are coming from. Just don't be dramatic and pretend to weep crocodile tears in a bid to show you really feel for the other person. That's totally undoing it.

10. Keep it Positive

When meeting people for the first time, always keep the conversation centered on positive subjects. Even when you feel that the other person is threading on a negative or controversial terrain, gently draw them back into a more positive conversation territory. Also, stick to subjects which most people in the group have a decent knowledge of. You're obviously not going to find a lot of takers if you start talking about stock market dynamics in a meditation class or group. Keep it positive to earn the other person's trust before getting them to do what you want them to.

Before they take the intended action or 'buy' from you, they have to 'buy' your trust and faith. This requires keeping it positive in the beginning to build the trust factor.

Stay with topics which offer minimal scope for disagreement, conflicts, and controversies. Keep it balanced and simple for a successful starting point conversation. If you annoy the other person at the beginning with a bunch of negative or controversial topics, they are likely to switch off and develop negative feelings towards you, something you don't want.

11. Body Language Speaks Volumes

Body language or non-verbal clues can probably convey much more than words. Send the right body language signals to create a more favourable impression and make yourself more likeable.

Tiny gestures like smiling frequently, nodding enthusiastically, lightly brushing your arm against the other person, maintaining constant eye contact, giving out a firm handshake, maintaining an energetic/peppy tone and other similar signals can go a long way in establishing a more likeable and influential persona. Remember – you don't get a second chance to make a first impression. Let every gesture count.

12. Do a Little Digging

A little background work goes a long creating a stunning first impression. Whether you are headed to a party or an important business networking event, keep a few topics ready after researching the group's predominant interest. For example, if you find out that the host or business associate/associates are heavily into spiritualism or travelling or cooking, research trending/buzzing topics in those niches to start an interesting conversation. This will help you fit into the group more effortlessly.

You'll be able to make the conversation livelier and draw people out of their awkwardness. Scan the day's newspapers for prominent headlines, go through book reviews, read up movie reviews and ratings or learn about the newest health trend doing the rounds of social media. These good to know topics resonate with most people and can help you appear well-informed and worldly-wise in front of a new audience.

If you know the names of people you will be meeting beforehand, you can track their social footprints across various social networks (just don't go about stalking them and making it obvious that you are checking out their profile every 2 minutes). It is easy to gauge people's interests, attitude and views through their social media profiles. This will give you a good indication about their likes and pet peeves, which can then be utilized for a striking a gainful conversation.

13. Build on Similarities

This is especially true while interacting with people from varied cultures and backgrounds. Find connecting bridges and build on it at every available opportunity. Find a common interest, favourite cuisine, a book you both particularly enjoyed reading or some other nice common ground.

Even if it something seemingly cheesy like wearing the same shirt/dress or shoes, always mention it to set a likeliness platform. Humans instantly take to people who are similar to them. When people realize your tastes or preferences are pretty much like them, they will be likelier to listen to you or look up to you.

14. Don't Overlook the Grooming

While you may be excellent conversationalist with flawless body language, few things can create a negative first impression like careless grooming. Even though this sounds basic, a lot of people consider it insignificant and focus on the "bigger things."

Never attend any social gathering without showering or styling your hair neatly. Maintain goof hygiene and grooming. Use a pleasant yet non overpowering fragrance. Keep a few mints handy in your bag. Sport a neat hair style (that doesn't keep distracting you), keep your nails well-manicured and teeth - sparkly white.

Wear clean and ironed clothes. It is surprising how many lose out simply because they fail to pay heed to these elementary aspects. Clothes and grooming add to your persona even before you begin speaking. Chances are, if you turn up poorly groomed, people may not even give you a chance to speak to them. Disorganized and untidy looking folks seldom influence others or act as role models by creating a favourable first impression.

15. Ditch the Greeting Awkwardness

Greeting people when you are introduced to them for the first time can be naturally awkward, especially if they belong to a different culture or region. You may be stumped about the appropriate greeting. Some people aren't comfortable even with a slight peck on the cheek, while others may not appreciate a lingering handshake. In such a scenario, it is safe to wait for the other person to make the first move. If they don't, keep it universal – smile your pearliest white, say hi/hello and offer a brief yet firm handshake.

Bonus – Tips for Detecting and Outsmarting Manipulation and Building Your Self-Esteem

Like it or wince, the world is full of wolves in sheep's clothing. You can't do much about pathological and emotional manipulators who are out to leverage your feelings and emotions to satisfy their wants. However, you can beat them at their own game by using a bunch of outsmarting techniques. Manipulation, if not recognized and handled efficiently, can tear down your sense of self worth and sanity. By recognizing and coping with manipulation, you are standing up for yourself and not allowing sinister manipulator's to fulfill their agenda by tramping on your feelings.

Here are some smart and effective hacks for outsmarting manipulators in their own game.

1. Put the spotlight on them by posing probing queries. Manipulators are constantly demanding things or making offers from their victims. As a victim, you will be made to feel that you need to prove yourself all the time. You'll often go out of the way to fulfill these demands. Stop. Each time you find them coming up with an unreasonable request, shoot back a few probing questions and shift the focus on them.

For example, does this seem like a legitimate and reasonable request to you?

Do you think what you've asked from me is fair or ethical?

Do I have the right to refuse?

Are you requesting or demanding that I do this?

What do I gain from doing this?

Are you really expecting that I will do this?

Are you reasonably justified in expecting me to do this?

Who stands to gain the most from this?

Basically, you are questions that show them the mirror, where they can witness their real sinister ploy. If the manipulator is self-aware or realizes that you've seen through their motives, they will most likely withdraw the request.

Manipulators try to put the focus on you as if you are unworthy or 'bad' if you don't do something for them. You've got to put the focus back on them by making them think if their request is indeed justified or reasonable, thus making them come across as people with evil motives.

Questions will eventually force the manipulator to realize that you are seeing through their game. The onus of the action will now shift from you to them.

For example, if you refuse the manipulator's request, the onus of justifying your action isn't on you. By asking probing questions, you are asking the manipulator to justify the reasonability of your request. So instead of feeling guilty about refusing something, you are making the manipulator realize that he/she is at fault for having unreasonable expectations.

Also, let your manipulator know that you don't accept being treated they way they treat you. Make it sufficiently clear that you don't appreciate their ways.

For instance, if you are already preoccupied with something and the manipulator makes a request to do something for them say something to the effect that, "I do not appreciate it when I am already working on something and you make another request of me before finish the current task."

Similarly when a person is trying to force you into making a decision that benefits them say something like, "I am able to make my own decisions and would really appreciate if you don't coerce me into making a decision in a hurry." You are being assertive and telling off your manipulator without being rude. You are simply standing up for your right and informing them that you have the right to take your time to decide, and it could backfire if they pressurize you into making a decision.

2. Take your time in fulfilling a request. Not only will manipulators make unreasonable requests, but they will also pressurize you into making a quick decision. They want to wield optimal control, influence, and pressure over you to get you to act in a specific way immediately. Manipulators realize that if you take more time, things may not go in their favor.

Do the exact opposite of what they want by taking more time. Sales people are always focused on closing the deal soon. Distance yourself from the manipulator's persuasion and take time to arrive at a decision. You don't have to act right away however much the person tries to pressurize you.

Take control over the person and situation by saying something like, "I'd like more time to think about it" or "it is my right to take more time to think about a decision as important as this" or "I need to evaluate the pros and cons before I arrive at a decision."

You can use this time to negotiate in your favor.

3. Say no assertively yet diplomatically. This is an art which will only come with practice. You don't want to offend the manipulator by saying a straight no. Yet, you want to be firm and let them know you won't allow them to walk over you. Stand your ground,

while still being polite and courteous. You don't have to feel guilty about your right to refuse an unreasonable request.

If you aren't up for something say, "I understand you want me to do this but I also feel I am not up for it right now. Another way to articulate your needs is, "what is the best thing for me to do right now is... One of the bets comebacks is to focus on your needs over those of the manipulator without guilt.

One of the sneakiest tricks used by manipulators is to make you feel guilty every time you don't comply with their request. When you stop feeling guilty about standing up for yourself or exercise your right to be treated with respect, manipulators become powerless.

4. Know your fundamental rights and worth. The most important weapon when you are dealing with manipulators is to know when your rights are being violated. You have the absolute right to stand up for those rights and defend yourself. You have the fundamental right to be treated with respect and honor.

Again, you have the right to express your emotions, needs, and feelings. You have the right to establish your priorities, refuse something without feeling guilty, the right to protect yourself/love ones from harm, the right to acquire what you pay for, and the right to live a happy, healthy and fulfilling life.

These are your boundaries and you can remind people to respect these rights. Psychological manipulators often want to take away your fundamental rights in a bid to exercise greater control over you. However, the power and authority to take charge of your life lies with you, and you shouldn't miss an opportunity to remind your manipulator that you alone are in control of your life. Distance yourself from people who do not respect these basic boundaries.

5. Maintain your distance. One of the most effective ways to spot a manipulator is by observing is they act differently with different folks or in diverse situations. Of course, we all come with some amount of social differential but if the person is habitually behaving out of character in extremes, he/she may be a master manipulator.

Think being unnaturally polite to one person and the next minute downright rudely to another or acting vulnerable one moment and then becoming aggressive within the next. When you witness this type of behavior, maintain your distance from the person. Avoid interacting with these people until absolutely necessary. You may end up inviting trouble. There are plenty of reasons people manipulate, and is very psychologically complex.

Don't attempt to fix manipulators all the time. It isn't your duty to change them. Just save yourself by moving on.

6. Avoid blaming yourself or personalization. One of the smoothest tricks used by manipulators is to make their victims feel like it is always their (the victim's) fault. Irrespective of what the manipulator does or knows, they will never take accountability for their faults. They will always blame the victim for all their wrongs.

As a victim of manipulation, you need to stop personalizing. The problem is not with you since you are simply being made to feel that it's your fault so you giveaway your rights to the manipulator and become powerless.

Do not be led into thinking that you are a problem or the problem lies with you. I knew a friend who was constantly chided by her husband for working hard to support the family. He never missed an opportunity to remind her that she wasn't a good wife or mother because she was always working. In her mind, she was working hard to give her children a great future (which really didn't make her a bad mother).

However, in his attempt to gain absolute control over her, he constantly blamed her and made her feel incompetent as a wife and mother. Initially, my friend believed everything that was told to her about being a bad mother and wife. However, over a period of time, she realized she was simply being blamed because her husband couldn't come to terms with his own shortcomings.

Ask yourself these questions before blaming yourself —

Are you being treated with respect?

Are the person's demands reasonable?

Do I feel good about myself while interacting with this person?

These are important clues about the real problem.

7. Set consequences for manipulative behavior. Psychological and pathological manipulators will always insist on disregarding your rights. They rarely take no for answer, offer flying into a rage or becoming aggressive. Recognize and state consequences clearly if they resort to aggression as a response to your refusal to comply with their unreasonable request.

An effectively communicated and asserted consequence can be used to pin down a manipulative person, and compel him/her to change their stand from violating your rights to respecting them. By reinforcing consequences, you are uncovering their hidden agendas and making them bring about a shift in their attitude towards you. Basically, you are strapping off their power.

It is important to stand up against the manipulator's bullying tactics. They will often try to scare you into giving in to their demands. Manipulators claim to hold on to your weaknesses to feel superior and powerful. If you stay passive and play along, they'll take greater advantage of you. Confront them and exercise your rights. Since manipulators are inherently cowardly, they'll retreat.

Research has proven that manipulative is closely linked to an abusive childhood or being victims of bullying. This in no way justifies the act of a bully. However, when you keep this in mind, you'll find healthier and more effective ways to respond to the manipulator.

8. Value yourself for who you are. Manipulators feed on the low self esteem of their victims. They'll always catch people who are vulnerable, unsure, low on confidence and don't know their real worth.

Rarely will the manipulator go after people with high self-esteem or sense of self-worth. If you can stay strong and take the manipulator head on by establishing your self-worth, it is evident you won't allow anyone to control you.

9. Silence is golden. Manipulators love drama. They will often provoke feelings of anger, fear, sadness and

more in you to think they've scored points over you. The best way to deal with this is to stay calm and practice deep breathing. Concentrate on your breath and how the body feels. Try to relax your muscles, and look the manipulator in their eye.

This simply body language of confidence and assertion can throw them off the tangent. A manipulator doesn't know how to deal with your calmness in such a situation. They are fully equipped to deal with your anger and fear. However, they don't expect you to react with calmness. It infuriates them and tells them the ploy doesn't seem to me effective on you. They will learn that emotions remain unchanged and shift to another target.

Don't get me wrong here. I am certainly not advocating giving up on a relationship at the first sign of manipulation. Manipulation can slowly pop up even in otherwise happy and fulfilling relationships, and it doesn't necessarily signify the end of a relationship. Before taking any drastic step, have a frank and open conversation with your partner or the person who is manipulating you. Gather the courage to ask them why they are doing this to you. These answers may give you vital clues into their state of mind and your next move.

If you've already attempted to have an open communication with your partner and they wouldn't have any of it, it may be time to explore other options such as therapy or counseling. However, you both have to be committed to the pursuit of overcoming manipulation within the relationship.

If nothing else works, you'll have to muster the courage to leave. I've seen people coming out of manipulative relationships through therapy, and they are not leading happier and more fulfilling lives. So it isn't like manipulation is the dead end for a relationship. If anything, use it as an opportunity to identify the flaws in your relationship mend these flaws gradually.

10. Practice self-care. Coping with a manipulation relationship can be intensely exhausting and stressful. Ensure you practice self-care to nurture your mind, body, and spirit, and don't let the manipulation take its toll on you. It is common to feel stressed at the end of each interaction with a manipulator (been there done that).

When you feel your mental energy drained after communication with a manipulator, do meditation, yoga or deep breathing. It infuses a sense of calm into your being. Do something enjoyable and exciting to prevent the negative feelings from spoiling your day. Go for a long walk in the midst of nature or talk to someone you trust.

Solid Tips For Increasing Your Self-Esteem

The core of being manipulated is experiencing feelings of incompetency and unworthiness. Rarely will you see confident people with high self esteem and high sense of self-worth being manipulated. Psychological manipulators thrive of making people feel unworthy and imbalanced. By inducing this feeling of insufficiency in their victims, they attempt to gain greater power and control over the victims, and in turn use their sense of powerlessness to fulfill selfish agendas.

One of the best ways to immunize yourself from manipulation is to develop high self-esteem and self-confidence. By having a high sense of self-worth and positive opinion about yourself, you are preventing hungry manipulators from sabotaging you.

Here are some powerful tips for increasing your overall self-esteem to make you less susceptible to manipulation.

1. Hold your inner critic. Yes, we all have that niggling inner frenemy who doesn't fail to remind us of how incapable we are at doing something or how miserable our life is compared to others. This inner voice shapes your thoughts and opinions about yourself.

Minimize your negative voice and consciously replace it with more positive and constructive terms. For instance, "I am so bad at this" can be replaced with "I may not be good at this but that shouldn't stop me learning everything I can about it and mastering it." You've just given a positive twist to a hopeless statement. Choose to use more hopeful, positive and inspiring words while speaking to yourself.

Stay stop loudly when you find your inner critic raring its monstrous head. You can also resort to a physical gesture like pinching yourself slowly or biting your lips each time you find your inner critic in hyper active mode.

2. Be more compassionate towards others people or treat them well. One of the best ways to raise your own self-esteem is to treat other people with greater compassion. When you make others feel good about themselves, you automatically feel great about yourself. When you treat people well, you inspire them to treat you well in return.

Practice kindness in your daily life by volunteering for a social cause (a huge self-esteem booster), hold the door for people, listen to someone vent out, let people pass through your lane while driving, buy coffee or treats for random people, encourage a person who is feeling deflated and similar other gestures. These will go a long way in building your self-esteem.

3. Try new things. People who are constantly trying new things or reinventing themselves are almost

always high on self-esteem. They are constantly challenging themselves by stepping outside their comfort zones. They try their hand at everything and appreciate various experiences, which increase feelings of competency. \

When you keep learning new things and developing your skills, you feel wonderful about yourself. You avoid falling into a rut. Keep trying a new adventure or picking up a new skill periodically. Nudge yourself to be active, passionate and productive. Set your spirit and soul into motion every now and then by taking up a hobby, picking a new skill or reading an inspiring book.

4. Avoid comparisons. You are slowly destroying yourself by constantly comparing yourself or your life with others. There is no victory in this, you'll always lose! It is a trap that will only make you feel more inadequate and unworthy.

Instead, look at where you were a few years ago and how far you've come to accomplish what you are today. Focus on your accomplishments and achievements today compared to a few years ago.

Albert Einstein famously said, "Everybody is a genius. But if you judge a fish by its ability to climb a tree, it will spend its whole life believing that it is stupid." Don't be that fish!

5. Spend time with positive people. Another great way to build your self-esteem is to surround yourself with people who support, encourage and inspire you. They should be people you look up to and should be able to influence you positively. It can be anyone from a professor to a mentor to a manager to a good friend.

Avoid interacting with people who focus on your flaws in try to bring to down on every available opportunity to feel superior about themselves. Look out for dream snatchers or people who laugh at your dreams or your ability to accomplish your goals. Self-esteem thrives in a positive environment in the midst of positive people. Be with people who make you feel good about yourself.

Also, be mindful of the books, websites and social media pages that you read. Let them charge your energy, not sap it. Don't read magazines that peddle unrealistic body images. Listen to podcasts that are naturally uplifting, empowering inspiring the next time you find yourself with some free time at hand. Watch television shows that uplift your spirit.

6. Sweat it out. Countless studies have established a high co-relation between exercise and healthy self-esteem. Exercise leads to enhanced mental and physical health, which in turn reduces stress and makes you feel good. It also brings more discipline into your life, which invariably increases self-esteem.

Exercise doesn't have to be boring. You can take up something fun and interesting like dance, cycling, swimming, aerobics, kickboxing and more. Anything that helps you sweat and gives you a small sense of accomplishment at the end. Physical activity boosts the secretion of endorphins within the brain, which makes us "feel good." And we all know how feeling good can have a positive effect on our self-perception and self-esteem.

7. Practice forgiveness. Is there some grudge that you've been holding for long? It may be related to an ex-partner, a family member during your growing up years, a friend who betrayed you or even yourself. Don't hold on to the feeling of bitterness. Overcome past feelings of shame, guilt, and regret, since holding on to it will only suck you further into the circle of negativity.

Conclusion

Thank you again for purchasing this book!

I hope it was able to help you to understand not just the ways through which people manipulate you but also powerful ways to manipulate people and immunize yourself against manipulation.

The next step is to simply use all the powerful strategies and techniques used in the book to understand manipulation techniques and prevent people from manipulating you in relationships, at work, and within your social circle. These manipulation strategies can be utilized effectively in our daily life to get people to do what we want them to.

There are plenty of practical tips, wisdom nuggets, and real life illustrations to help you gain a solid understanding of how manipulation works and how it can be used in your everyday life.

Lastly, if you enjoyed this book, then I'd like to ask you for a favor, would you be kind enough to leave a review for this book? It'd be greatly appreciated!

Thank you and good luck!

www.ingramcontent.com/pod-product-compliance
Lightning Source LLC
Chambersburg PA
CBHW070527010526
44110CB00050B/2175